SHALOM

PAUL CLAYTON **GIBBS**

HOW TO **REACH**
ANYONE ANYWHERE

Part of the Ancient Trilogy

Shalom: How to Reach Anyone Anywhere
Copyright © 2019 by Paul Clayton Gibbs

Published by Harris House Publishing
harrishousepublishing.com
Colleyville, Texas
USA

This title is available in other formats.
978-1-946369-50-5
978-1-946369-49-9

Cover creation by Andrew Sherrington | David Lamprecht | design by Paul Clayton Gibbs
Author's photo by Lena Gresser
Production team: Terry Tamashiro Harris | André Lopes | Megan Freiwald | Matthew Harris

All Scripture quotations, unless otherwise indicated, are taken from the Holy Bible, *New International Version®*, NIV®. Copyright ©1973, 1978, 1984, 2011 by Biblica, Inc.™ Used by permission of Zondervan. All rights reserved worldwide. www.zondervan.com. The "NIV" and "New International Version" are trademarks registered in the United States Patent and Trademark Office by Biblica, Inc.™

Scripture quotations marked NLT are taken from the Holy Bible, New Living Translation, copyright ©1996, 2004, 2007, 2013, 2015 by Tyndale House Foundation. Used by permission of Tyndale House Publishers, Inc., Carol Stream, Illinois 60188. All rights reserved.

Scripture quotations marked OJB are taken from The Orthodox Jewish Bible. Copyright ©2011 by AFI International. Used by permission. All rights reserved.

Scripture quotations marked KJV are from The King James Version. The KJV is public domain in the United States.

Scripture quotations marked ISV are taken from the Holy Bible: International Standard Version®. Copyright © 1996-forever by The ISV Foundation. ALL RIGHTS RESERVED INTERNATIONALLY. Used by permission.

Cataloging-in-Publication Data

Gibbs, Paul Clayton, 1964 -
    Shalom: How to Reach Anyone Anywhere / Paul Clayton Gibbs
        p.cm
    Includes biographical references
    ISBN 978-1-946369-50-5 (pbk.)
    1. Christian Ministry. 2. Evangelism. I. Title.
BS1235.2.G53   2019

                                                                                                                                       2019942987

All rights reserved. No portion of this book may be reproduced, stored in a retrieval system, or transmitted in any form or by any means—electronic, mechanical, photocopy, recording, or any other—except for brief quotation in printed reviews, without the prior permission of the publisher.

This book is dedicated to

The people of peace.

To the many Pais hosts around the world. Thank you for opening your homes and hearts to our young missionaries.

To our partnering churches. Thank you for seeing the importance of the mission and making His Kingdom your primary concern.

To those who support our work. May God bless you for the prayers and sacrifices that give us the strength to do what we do.

Together we make missionaries who make missionaries.

#shalom

DOWNLOAD THE SHALOM TEMPLATE AT mypais.com

Contents

SHALOM
Why?......................10
What?....................16
How?......................19

SPREAD
Why?......................24
What?....................32
How?......................39

SPOT
Why?......................48
What?....................55
How?......................64

STAY
Why?......................74
What?....................80
How?......................89

SEND
Why?......................100
What?....................106
How?......................113
Strategy.................122

SOURCES
Shalom Template......128
Endnotes.................130

SHALOM

Peace in a polarized world

SHALOM TEMPLATE

Step 1 - Spread

The Principle: Spread and do not decide in advance who will respond.
The Practice: Offer a unique experience of the Kingdom.

The Questions:
1. What is my Box?
2. What unique experience of the Kingdom can I offer?

Step 2 - Spot

The Principle: Spot the people of peace.
The Practice: Provide a next step.

The Questions:
3. What is the truth they already accept?
4. What next step will build upon it?

Step 3 - Stay

The Principle: Stay and disciple the people of peace.
The Practice: Continue with them by layering their experience.

The Questions:
5. What are the gaps in their understanding?
6. How can I broaden their experience?

Step 4 - Send

The Principle: Send them to those who first sa d no.
The Practice: Equip them to reach anyone, anywhere.

The Questions:
7. Where can I first go with them?
8. What can I equip them with?

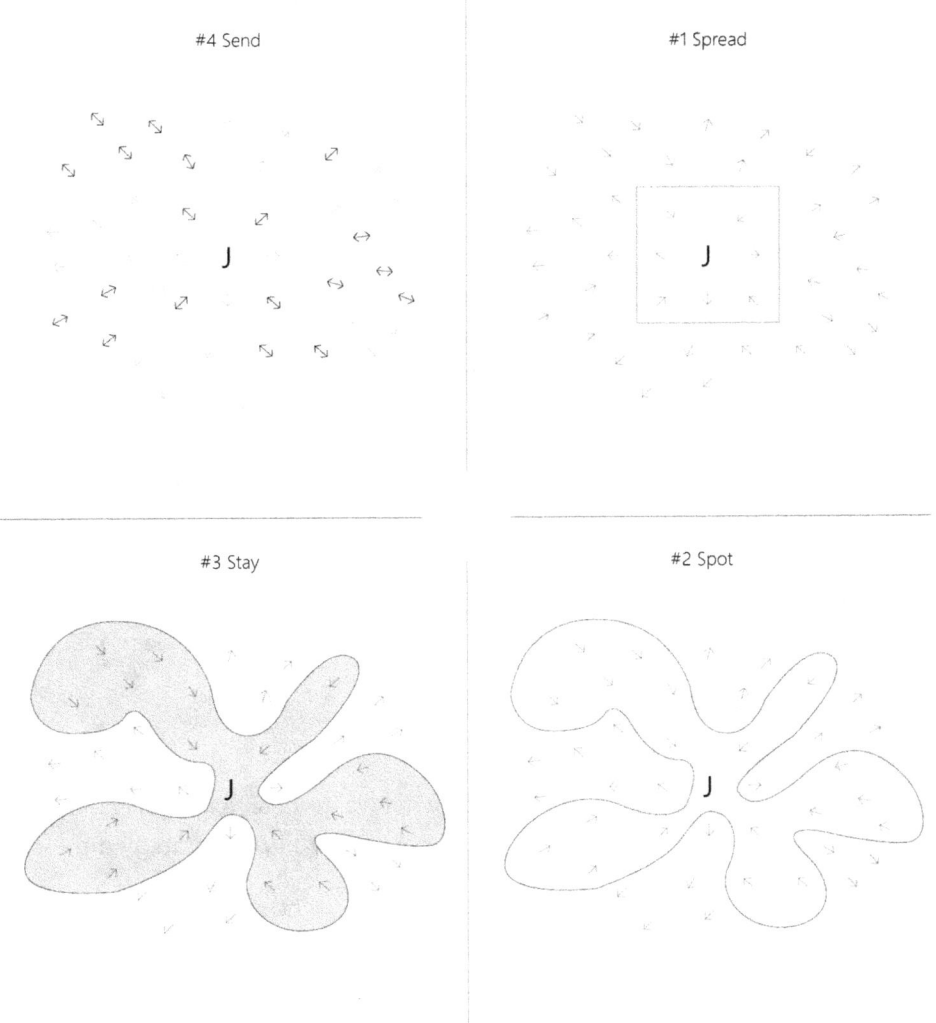

Why?

Invitation

My method of evangelism changed when I started asking a different question.

Not long after my wife and I moved into our first house in Manchester, England, a national newspaper labelled our block of four streets "a ghetto of underprivileged underachievers," and around that same time the local government sent a small trifold pamphlet to fourteen thousand local residents about a young boy named Robert. The pamphlet detailed his ASBO (anti-social behavior order) and listed the petty crimes he had committed and the nuisance he had caused. It displayed a small map of our neighborhood detailing Robert's 'no-go zone,' the area in which he was forbidden to set foot without authorized supervision. Essentially, he had been placed under house-arrest.

One section was titled, *What You Can Do to Help*.

Eagerly, I scanned the paragraph to see what we as local residents could do to support both his family and the local community. What strategy did the City Council have?

> "If you see Robert break his ASBO, please contact the police, or the Council's local housing service, safe in the knowledge that we will protect your privacy."[1]

The answer was clear: they had no plan. If we saw Robert entering his restricted zone, we were to simply make an anonymous phone call and he would presumably receive further punishment. Although the text of the pamphlet filled its six sections, I could summarize the whole thing in three words:

"We . . . give . . . up!"

Yet, Jesus gives up on no one.

In His mind, no one is unreachable! And for His disciples, a 'no-go zone' cannot exist. Yet the transformational benefits of knowing Jesus were hidden from Robert and his family because, along with the vast majority of the UK's population, they were never likely to step foot inside a church building. This breaks my heart, because my vision is that everyone will have a chance to taste and see that God is good. So when I see a society looking for answers and a Church unsure of how to enter it, it galvanizes me. Finding a way to bring the Gospel of peace into a broken world is a path I have been on since I first came to know Jesus, and Robert's pamphlet helped me discover a way forward. Or, at least, a template from which to work out a way forward. That trifold leaflet prompted me to ask a question I had never heard anyone ask before:

> Why do we spend so much of our time, energy, and resources *inviting* people . . . when Jesus spent so much of His *getting Himself invited?*

While I regularly pray that the Roberts of this world will learn the value of coming to church, God's desire is that the churches of this world will learn the value of going to Robert. The briefest examination of Jesus's methods reveal that He knew the benefits of getting Himself invited by others to share His message in their world and on their terms. We see Him do this multiple times in very subtle ways and occasionally quite blatantly:

> *When Jesus reached the spot, he looked up and said to him, "Zacchaeus, come down immediately. I must stay at your house today." So he came down at once and welcomed him gladly.*[2]

However, in all the conferences I have attended and all the sermons I have heard, little instruction has been given in how to do this. Which begs the further question . . .

Have we as the Church lost the art of *getting ourselves invited*?

And how can we rediscover it?

Benefits

First, let me say, I am *not* proposing that "How do we invite people?" is the wrong question.

One week before my fourteenth birthday, I heard the Gospel for the first time when I was invited to a 'Tent Crusade' in the middle of a field. Although I spent much of the evening confused by what was going on around me, I became a follower of Jesus that night. I know the power of an invitation. So, in my mind, to say that the question, "How can we attract people to a building or an event?", is in some way wrong, ineffective, or outdated is to be foolish, naive, and deluded. Church is more effective when it is attractive. However, when we explore only methods of inviting people, we ask only half of the questions we should be asking . . . and, therefore, discover only half of the answers available to us. And, in my opinion, it is the least effective half!

Here are some benefits I have found in getting myself invited:

Your message, when invited, reaches far more people.

In 1988 I got myself invited into the UK school system. I will share how I did this later, but for now let me just point out a simple statistic. At that time, our church had around 20 to 30 teenagers attending the youth program. By being welcomed as a guest into local public high schools, however, I was able to share my faith with around 10,000 students per academic year. This included ministering to several hundred of them on a weekly basis and eventually integrating a great many into the Church.

Your message, when invited, is seen as helpful, not hurtful.

I found that, by using the template Jesus modeled, I did not need to force my way into schools, coerce people, or resort to any legal or political threats. Once in the classroom, I was prompted by both staff and students to share my faith on a regular basis. Rather than being viewed as a nuisance, weirdo, or pest, I was seen as a friend, advisor, and associate.

Your message, when invited, is more socially acceptable.

I also discovered a worldwide principle. Always staying within the rules and etiquette of the secular schools I entered, I found that if I was responding to a question asked by a student, sharing my beliefs became a perfectly acceptable practice. Thirty years later, the organization I lead reaches into schools, businesses, and other institutions on six continents. Our practice within the Pais Movement is to come alongside the local church as a missionary outfitter, providing them with the people and programs to incorporate new methods of evangelism, discipleship, and Bible Study. We have a charter of conduct and, in that charter, we promise to abide by the legal parameters of the schools we serve.[3] The same goes for the other institutes into which we get invited. Within those boundaries, we have found that, from Ireland to Islamabad, if our teams follow the rabbinic model we teach them and prompt the questions they want to be asked, then their message is seen as both relevant and appropriate.

Your message, when invited, is more credible.

In schools, my presentations always benefited from the kudos and credibility of whoever welcomed me. Although I would often start with a disclaimer, the reality is that my hearers would still see me as a member of the faculty and, therefore, what I taught carried a certain professional authority.[4] Whether you are being invited by a tax collector, school principal, or a respected CEO, being invited gives what you say more oomph!

Your message, when invited, is less expensive than when you invite them.

Getting yourself invited makes economic sense. I once wrote about a visit I made to a youth ministry venue in Oklahoma.[5] The building was epic, contemporary and kitted out in the latest technology. The reception area was a work of art. The snack bar was as good as any you might find in a movie theatre. There was a basketball court, entirely encased in glass. On the second level were rows of iPods (still a novelty at that time) and rows of the latest game consoles. As a place to attract young people, it could not have been better designed for its time. However, from a purely missional point of view, that building reflected the economic disadvantage of a purely 'inviting' methodology. I dread to think how much money it must have cost to build and then maintain! Yet I was told that the maximum attendance possible was 1,200 teenagers at an outreach event on a Wednesday night. That is minuscule when you consider how many young people attend schools in that community.

Getting yourself invited is much less costly because someone else has bought the building, foot the bills, and paid the staff. Getting myself invited meant I could just show up and do my thing.

So did Jesus, and so can you!

Your message, when invited, also teaches others how to share it.

For me, this might be the greatest of all the benefits. Many years ago, a young man approached me with a problem. He had recently started to follow Christ, and many of his work colleagues were now eager to know why his behavior had changed. He could reiterate the soundbites he heard at church but found they did not resonate with his colleagues. As my friend was struggling to share the Gospel in that environment, he asked me the following question:

> "How can I get my colleagues to church in order to hear you speak?"

Now, the likelihood of them traveling across the city to step into church for the first time was not impossible, but it was definitely off-putting for them. I asked him how much he was willing to pay for them to hear the Gospel. He replied that he would give almost anything . . . but agreed to approximately $20 per person. So at their next office social event in a nearby restaurant, he picked up each person's $20 tab and I was invited to be the after-dinner speaker. Everyone knew that I was there to explain his faith in fifteen minutes. By the end of a fun evening, not only had his colleagues heard the Gospel but, just as importantly, I was able to fulfill the responsibility of any Christian leader:

So Christ himself gave (leaders), to equip his people for works of service.[6]

Watching me, he learned how he could communicate the message of Jesus using language applicable to his work environment.

These are just some of the added benefits of getting yourself invited to share your faith on their turf. It's less confrontational, less costly, more effective, more credible, and more productive when it comes to reproducing our God given talents in others.

So what's stopping us?

What?

Polarized

Let's face it, when the world has a party, its first thought is rarely:

"Hey, let's invite the Christians!"

Maybe that is never meant to be. And yet Jesus was often welcomed by those seeking answers. But are we? Do we feel our only option is to either entice people into our world or force ourselves into theirs?

Personally, I have become disturbed by the way some of my Christian brothers and sisters communicate their faith via social media. I often wonder if some posts are really intended to help create a conversation with those of a different view, or if instead we are merely playing to our base as politicians often do? When we publish our Bible quotes, soundbites, or thoughts, what is our end-game?

To win more souls or to win more retweets?

Many Christians realize we are in a spiritual battle, and yet scoring points in the 'culture wars' is to no advantage if we are losing souls. So what stops us from getting ourselves invited in an increasingly polarized world? Well, to start, perhaps we have never really understood the truth of an old adage:

Art beats an argument.

There is an 'art' to evangelism. Do it well and you get to paint a picture of the Kingdom of God in someone else's life. Do it poorly and you end up demanding an opportunity to push your opinions on those unwilling to pull them from you. Jesus demonstrated the skill of getting Himself invited into His world, a world far more polarized than ours today.

For us to do the same, we must understand how *shalom* shaped His methods.

Peace

Jesus came to bring peace.

Now before you jump out of your chair, I know He said just the opposite:

> *"I did not come to bring peace, but a sword."*[7]

However, we have to understand that Jesus, quoting Micah 7, was not talking about an *intentional* desire to bring war, but was instead referring to the *incidental* collateral damage that comes from bringing peace between man and God. He was attacking passivity . . . the desire to avoid rocking someone's boat . . . even if their boat is sinking.

Shalom is the Hebrew word for peace and is rooted in the term *'shaleim,'* which means *completion*. Although used for both 'hello' and 'goodbye,' it implies a blessing much greater and more profound than a simple greeting. As one Jewish scholar puts it:

> "We call it peace but it means far more than mere peace of mind or a cease-fire between enemies. In the Bible, *shalom* means universal flourishing . . . *Shalom*, in other words, is the way things ought to be."[8]

But is bringing peace, a sense of completion, what we are known for?

Sometime ago I met a Christian friend of mine for a meal. On the way out of the restaurant, we were greeted by a couple of men who knew him well and they began chatting together. Early in the conversation, they told my friend of their recent visit to Europe and, in a vulgar fashion, began to divulge how sensual and attractive they found some of the young ladies. Immediately my friend shut down the conversation.

> "We are Christians. We don't talk that way. Great to see you . . . Goodbye!"

A few seconds later, we were out of the restaurant. I was initially unsure what I thought about this. My first reaction was one of admiration. I know many Jesus followers who would have smiled awkwardly at the men and, by their non-confrontation, condoned their derisive objectivity of women. To his immense credit, my friend was willing to bring God into the situation. He clearly understood what Jesus meant in the Sermon on the Mount when He said, "Blessed are the peace-*makers,*" and not, "Blessed are the peace-*keepers.*" Jesus's blessing does not apply to the man who sees two of his friends fighting and will not step in because they may turn on him. Neither does He apply His blessing to those who will not say what a friend needs to hear in order to avoid upsetting them. That is a peace-*keeper*. Peace-*makers*, however, will risk their friendships in order to serve their friends. They step in because their desire for people to be brought into God's peace is stronger than their own love for a peaceful life. Therefore, may I suggest that:

> The greatest lovers of people are those who love God more than they love people!

My friend had shown the courage of his convictions and, in spite of the possibility of losing their friendship, he wore his faith with integrity.

However . . . if behavior modification is our goal, then this may have been a great move. But is it? If spiritual transformation is our objective, helping others find *completion* in God, then was what he did the best option? After all, the conversation was immediately halted, not by them, but by us. There was no progression of the Gospel in their lives, never mind any completion. In my personal experience, the vast majority of Christians are similar to my friend, not judgmental, but full of grace. Yet they limit the opportunity to bring *shalom* because the Church is poor at teaching us how to bring peace to a polarized world. My friend did the best he could do with the tools he had been given . . . but Jesus may have handled it differently.

Let's take a look at His example.

How?

Plan

If only Christ had given us a clear strategy for mission!

Well, He did.

Jesus first modeled and then taught it to His disciples who carried it on throughout the Gospels. We see Paul the Apostle later adopt Christ's methodology as he reached into Europe.[9] It is reproducible, and once you recognize it, you will see it time and again in the life of Jesus, the book of Acts, and several of the epistles. It can be observed as a fragmented mosaic throughout the Gospels, but it is most clearly seen as a step-by-step process four times within the synoptic Gospels.[10] The most comprehensive example is found in Luke 10.

> *After this the Lord appointed seventy others and sent them two by two ahead of him to every town and place where he was about to go. He told them . . . "Go! I am sending you out like lambs among wolves. Do not take a purse or bag or sandals; and do not greet anyone on the road. When you enter a house, first say, 'Peace to this house.' If someone who promotes peace is there, your peace will rest on them; if not, it will return to you. Stay there, eating and drinking whatever they give you, for the worker deserves his wages. Do not move around from house to house. When you enter a town and are welcomed, eat what is offered to you. Heal the sick who are there and tell them, 'The kingdom of God has come near to you.' But when you enter a town and are not welcomed, go into its streets and say, 'Even the dust of your town we wipe from our feet as a warning to you.'"*[11]

I have taken Jesus's *modus operandi* and broken it down into four steps:

Spread. Spot. Stay. Send.

This book unpacks that plan. It is a guideline for evangelism but must be followed with flexibility. As you will see, the four steps can often overlap and blur into each other; during any one of them a person might make Jesus Lord of their life. Yet, you will also notice that each step builds upon the one before it, creating a mission plan that has both depth and sustainability. And, it and can be used on both a personal and organizational level.

Template

My hope is that this book will help us reexamine our approach to bringing peace with God to a polarized world. As with the other two books in the *Ancient Trilogy*, which look at discipleship and Bible study, the aim of *Shalom* is not to convince you of its worth with an over reliance on statistics or data. It is instead a plea to return to what Jesus did and a belief that the 'proof is in the pudding.' My hope is that you will put its contents into practice and, in doing so, experience that what Jesus modeled really works! Similarly to the other two books, I have taken what Jesus did 2,000 years ago and presented it in a unique, practical template using diagrams and simple questions that can be applied across multiple scenarios.

The book is divided into sections that cover the four steps: Spread. Spot. Stay. Send. Each of the four steps are then outlined in three distinct chapters:

In *Why?* I explain the philosophy that guided Jesus.

In *What?* I provide a template to help practice each step.

In *How?* I help you apply that template to your own situation.

There are many great books on how to invite others. This is not one of them. It should not be seen as competition to those books, but as a companion to them. It is meant to help us go *beyond* what we already know, *how to invite people*, and develop new methods in order to get ourselves invited. I pray that it will help you in the same way it helped me even as I was writing it.

I began its compilation when two of my neighbors asked me to help plant a church in the small community where we had recently moved. This gave me an excellent opportunity to apply the template while helping to lead a fledgling Christian fellowship. I finished the book around eighteen months later when we had raised up a pastor to take over the church comprised of nearly a hundred of our neighbors. The template has also helped me in other forms of evangelism. I have used it in my personal evangelism, as a youth and community worker, as the director of an international missions organization, and in pioneering new churches and repurposing old ones. In that time, I have found that what Jesus did 2,000 years ago still works today!

For some of you, this book will change the way you think about mission. In fact, the template it unpacks may influence the way you pursue any kind of relationship. For others, its steps may not be revolutionary, but may give you words and a structure for what you are already doing, and thereby provide a training tool for you to teach others. Whether you are new to evangelism or an experienced Christian leader, I expect you will find some interesting twists and turns along the way.

As a case study that the majority of readers may be familiar with, I will unpack the template using a local church scenario. Added to this, I will share from my personal experience how the template has helped me reach young people in schools all over the world. For each step, I have integrated what I have called the 'POP chart' in order to help you visualize the process.[12]

In doing this, my aim is to help *anyone* reach *anyone else* . . . *anywhere!*

SPREAD

Spread and do not decide
in advance who will respond

Why?

Nuance

I doubt you need me to convince you that we should reach as many souls as possible. However, I do want to address the question of why we don't and then share the part of the template that may help us avoid it.

The first time I was ever invited by someone else into a public high school, I was a raw recruit. A friend had asked me to assist him as he presented six lessons leading up to Easter. The initial lesson went so well that the school's principal asked if my friend would teach twice as many students the following week. He told her that would not be a problem and said:

> "Paul can teach one-half of the group simultaneously as I teach the other . . . Can't you, Paul?"

Blindsided, I nodded. I was assured that I would get a full set of notes and be trained in advance. The following week I received no training and only fifteen minutes worth of material for the hour-long presentation. I had to create the rest of the plan on my own. The week after, my friend informed me that he could no longer commit to the rest of the series and asked if I could take it over. I was given titles but absolutely no material. I was asked to prepare and then present two lessons per week for four more weeks. I was untrained, ill equipped, and terrified . . . Wouldn't you be?

But what went through my mind was this:

> *"If I don't take this opportunity to tell these teenagers about Jesus, who will?"*

However, if I had been raised in today's Christian culture, would I have asked a different question . . .

"Is this my ministry?"

I wonder if this is the result of a me-centric Gospel?

In the Church's desire to offer people a personal relationship with Jesus, have we lost sight of the big picture? If so, what are the consequences? Over the last twenty-five years as I've recruited wave after wave of young adults to reach young people, I have noticed that our new applicants seem to be losing sight of a faith that is to be shared and replacing it with one that can be shelved if the need does not fit the narrative of their personal vision. This is not a result of 'millennialism' but of Church culture.

To what might I compare this mindset?

It is like the captain of a small boat that comes across the Titanic. Upon seeing the men, women, and children drowning in the dark and freezing waters, he begins to motor forward in order to rescue them. Then he stops . . . *Hang on a minute!* he thinks to himself. *What kind of boat do I have?*

Is this a fishing boat?

Might it be a tugboat?

What if it is a pleasure boat?

And while he is pondering what kind of vessel he has, the people drown in a watery grave.

Why? Because he forgot that, first and foremost, his boat was a boat! So it is when we forget that God's mission is to be our primary concern and that our 'ministry gifts' are little more than nuance.

God is calling all of us to something bigger than any of us!

Schmooze

I believe Jesus was very aware of a similar problem with the seventy missionaries He sent out. He was concerned that their personal agendas would limit those they could potentially reach. This is the reason Jesus added what initially seems to be a superfluous requirement to the first stage of His template:

> "... and do not greet anyone on the road."[13]

Several commentaries suggest this instruction was given because greetings could be too time-consuming and delay the message. This would make sense, especially if there were some kind of Jewish custom that meant a greeting lasted much longer than it would today. So I checked to see if that was the case.

It wasn't.

A greeting then was pretty much the same as it would be now. The idea that Jesus was urging His disciples to get to their destination as fast as they could does not hold water. In fact, it would be contrary to His personal example. Just think about how often He allowed His own journey to be delayed in order to advance the Kingdom of God in someone else's life. No, in reality, Jesus had adopted this command from the ancient Hasidim who predated Jesus and commanded their disciples that while on their mission, *"Even if the King greets a man, he must not return the greeting."*[14] His instruction was less to do with speed and more to do with intention.[15]

According to Jewish commentary, a more accurate understanding of Jesus's instruction would be that He was warning His disciples not to *schmooze* along the way![16] To schmooze, a Yiddish phrase, is a custom that is understood by most of us. It means:

> To press flesh, to win people over, to charm.

A contextual interpretation might be 'to network for personal benefit.'

To reach more people, we also must avoid schmoozing. And schmoozing can come in various forms.

During 1988, the Prime Minister of the United Kingdom declared that all public schools should have a "daily act of broadly Christian worship."[17] Every campus in the UK had to have some kind of prayer, hymn, or religious homily once a day for the entire school. Teaching staff that felt uncomfortable fulfilling this obligation were encouraged to outsource the opportunity to others in the community. That meant that the government gave every church in England, Wales, Scotland and Northern Ireland the chance to reach almost every young person in the country . . . five days a week![18]

I would love to tell you that the UK Church flooded the schools with both resources and people to fulfill this need. However, over the last 30 years, with some exceptions, we have done relatively little when compared to the incredible opportunity given to us. In the UK, only 5% of young people ever attend a church and far less attend regularly, yet few churches have any kind of realistic schools outreach program.[19] God has put an opportunity to disciple an entire generation right under our noses and we are blowing it!

Why?

Is the church too lazy? Apathetic? Disinterested? No, not at all. The UK church as a whole is hardworking, passionate, and very concerned about the youth of our nation. We are not snoozing, we are schmoozing! So caught up have we become in building our churches and attracting people to our Sunday services that we have not put anything like the comparative effort or resources into the opportunity God has put before us. It is of course much easier to lament the lack of God in schools than to allow God to school our methods.

Unintentionally, we've allowed our personal ministry goals to blind us to an open door.

At the very beginning, Christ was concerned that His disciples may be so tempted to use their newfound position to further their personal goals. It is likely that the temptation He was most concerned about was their desire for even greater status, something upon which they appeared to fixate.[20] Maybe they would be tempted to use the opportunity of being His herald to gain a more prestigious position but commit to a lesser cause? I have felt this temptation. There have been times when I have been offered an alternative job in Christian ministry with a larger salary than I make in my role with Pais. However, when I have analyzed those opportunities, they often result in me having less of an impact for His Kingdom than I presently have. In those times, Jesus's command rings in my ears and I feel challenged to answer with a paraphrase of John's words:

I must become less so He can reach more.[21]

The Judaic interpretation, 'do not schmooze,' makes even more sense when you consider Christ's further instruction: *"Do not move around from house to house."*[22] This key statement is again a challenge to refrain from seeking out a better situation for ourselves at the detriment of more effective outreach. However, the best evidence we have that Jesus was warning His disciples not to schmooze is seen *after* they returned:

> *Then the seventy returned with joy, saying, "Lord, even the demons are subject to us in Your name."*
>
> *And He said to them, "I saw Satan fall like lightning from heaven. Behold, I give you the authority to trample on serpents and scorpions, and over all the power of the enemy, and nothing shall by any means hurt you. Nevertheless do not rejoice in this, that the spirits are subject to you, but rather rejoice because your names are written in heaven."*[23]

Why did Jesus appear to pour cold water on His disciples' enthusiasm?

When we apply the second level of Haverim Devotions to this passage, we uncover something interesting.[24] Using *r'mez*, a Hebraic teaching technique, Jesus was invoking Isaiah 11:8: *"The infant will play near the hole of the cobra, and the young child put his hand into the viper's nest."*[25] Jesus was bringing to the disciples' minds the whole of Isaiah 11 which contains a description of the branch of Jesse and of the coming Kingdom. So what was His point?

He was reminding them of the big picture!

The disciples had become excited about the wrong thing. They were more thrilled by their ministry than His mission. Jesus knew this would be a temptation all along and was starting the process of recalibrating their mindset even as He sent them out. Bringing *shalom* requires that we find a way to give *everyone* the chance to respond, not filtering out people by limiting our mission to what suits us best or putting things in place that do not need to be there. So, whether the temptation is ambition, comfort, status, or wealth, the first stage of the Shalom Template keeps us from inadvertently limiting those who can respond. In doing so, it provides a practical key for more effective outreach.

At the time that the UK government afforded us the opportunity to reach students in schools, we celebrated. Yet four decades later, are we still allowing our preoccupation with church programs to minimize our opportunity for greater Kingdom impact? If so, we may be on the edge of losing yet another generation. Sadly, few doors stay open permanently.

What's stopping you from walking through yours?

Invisible

Before we look at the practical steps to reaching more people, let's briefly examine our own hearts and mindset to see if any invisible agendas or principles hinder us. To start that thought process, here are some examples of schmoozing I have witnessed.

We might put a person before people.

I wholeheartedly subscribe to the idea that we should not put a program before a person. However, I also believe that we should not put a person before people. Occasionally we may limit those we could reach because we do not want to upset or antagonize an individual, preferring to keep them on our side. I remember witnessing a schools worker literally cry in front of a group of ministers because another group of youth workers wanted to serve in his city. He saw this new group as potential competition rather than possible collaborators. The church ministers of the city succumbed to what in essence was emotional blackmail and thousands of students received a reduced chance of hearing the Gospel. His insecurities were put before the eternal security of the teenagers. In that same way, we as individuals must not, for any reason, give in to the pressure of the few when we have the opportunity to reach the many! Have you ever done that? Are you doing that right now?

We may put our comfort above the Gospel.

Many of us can become so comfortable caring for those we have already reached that we downsize our effort to reach others. I once saw research on the 'Seventy-Year Cycle' that highlighted how some churches struggle to maintain growth.[26] The reason given is that the questions which drive the leadership in the first stages of a new church plant are, "Why are we here?" and "Who are we here for?" These are later replaced by the question, "How do we keep who we have?" Focusing on this third question to the detriment of the first two leads to church attendance plateauing and then declining. The principle is clear: we must never stop *spreading* and reaching new people. Perhaps you could take a moment to ask yourself if you have already settled? Do you give far more attention to those you have reached than those you could reach?

We can put our politics above the Gospel.

Many of us have developed specific values that we want to pass on to those we reach. However, Christ's commission is not a license to convert others to our political viewpoint. Have you added appendages to the Gospel that could limit people's willingness to accept Jesus's core message? Do you only want people in your church who vote and see life the way you do?

We might put our brand above the Gospel.

This week *The Times* newspaper reported that the clothing company Burberry destroyed $38 million worth of extra stock by fire.[27] Why? To protect their brand. Instead of giving their clothes to those in need, they saw the value of their logo as more important. Personally, I find that disturbing, and so it also makes me sad to see people or groups that could work together neglect to do so because they want a project or outreach to carry their specific church name.

Will you work with others . . . even if they receive the benefit of attracting those who respond and you do not?

We sometimes put our skill-set above the Gospel.

The first opportunity I was given in one particular school was not the one I really wanted. It was an assembly where I was asked to speak to several hundred non-religious high school students about the Day of Pentecost. At the time, I had no idea why they asked me to speak on this subject. I was told that I could not use humor, object lessons, or any visual images. Due to these restrictions, it was not the ideal opportunity to use my gifts, but it was something they felt I could do uniquely better than anyone else in their school. I thought my talk was relatively boring, but the teachers loved it. It turned out to be a test! Afterwards, I discovered that they simply wanted to know if they could trust me to stick within guidelines and if I could keep the students engaged. As I stepped off the stage, a department head immediately offered me a series of lessons to teach on Christianity. This was not the last time I was given a damage-limitation test to pass.

If you are too narrow in the steps that you take, you may miss getting your foot in the door. And if you miss out on that, how will you be able to provide a broader and deeper experience of the Kingdom?

Now that we have checked our hearts and minds, let's get practical . . .

What?

Kerusso

The first step in the Shalom Template is simple:

> Spread and do not decide in advance who will respond.

Specifically, this is how Jesus commanded them:

> *After this the Lord chose seventy others. He sent them out two together to every city and place where He would be going later.*[28]

Although this verse may at first sound rather generic, I believe Jesus was intentionally giving them a very particular instruction. He wanted them to go into *every* town, giving *every* person living there the opportunity to receive them and their message. Without this precise instruction, they may have either decided in advance who would respond or even who they *wanted* to respond. In doing so, they would have put a self-imposed limit on their mission. There was of course precedent for Jesus's concern. Remember the story of Jonah, a man given a divine message but who felt he could decide who should get to hear it and who should not?[29] Neither must we 'play God' with people's eternal lives.

So let's take a look at the first stage of the POP diagram. Here we can see many arrows pointing in the direction of Jesus and many pointing away from Him. The arrows represent people. Those moving *towards* Jesus are searching Him out with a desire to know more about His Kingdom. Those who are moving *away* from Jesus may have no interest in God or have lost interest in Him.

SPREAD

Jesus sent His disciples with a proclamation, or *kerusso*:[30]

> "... Heal the sick who are there and tell them, 'The kingdom of God has come near to you.'"[31]

Importantly, the commission was to offer *everyone* the opportunity to not just hear about the Kingdom of God but *experience* it. This opportunity to *'taste and see'* was crucial to Christ's strategy of bringing *shalom*. He believed when people *experienced* the Kingdom of Heaven, it would lead them to invite His disciples to do an even greater work in their lives and in their world.

So, if the principle in first step of the Shalom Strategy is:

> Spread and do not decide in advance who will respond!

How do we put that principle into practice?

> We offer a unique experience of the Kingdom of God.

Essentially, we want people to experience God's Kingdom at work in their own world without having to first come into ours. Our hope is that they will then invite us into their world to a greater degree, becoming His disciples and continuing the pattern of missionaries making missionaries.

So now we must factor in one of the biggest obstacles to doing this ...

The *Box*.

Box

The Box is the way that we determine in advance who gets to hear the message and who does not. That is rarely the intention of our Box, but it is a result of it. It represents a system of some kind and can be a result of schmoozing in one form or another. t might be a structure, a methodology, a framework, or even a mindset that we inadvertently put before reaching more people. For instance, if the Box represents a local church structure, what do you notice in the diagram below?

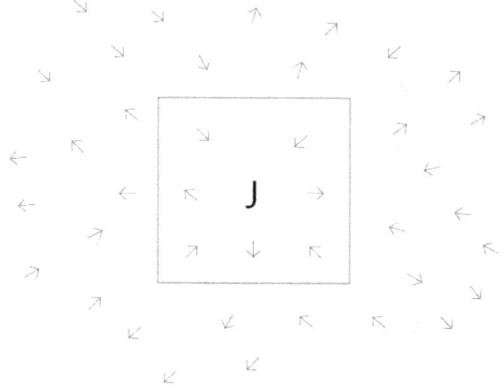

There are more arrows *outside* the Box than in it.

To 'Spread' is to offer as many as possible inside *and* outside the Box an opportunity to *experience* the Kingdom of God. For some churches, however, the people to whom they offer an experience of God are primarily those within their structures—people who attend a Sunday morning service or an event the church hosts. It is not that these churches do not have any form of outreach but, as I will explain later, they may not be offering experiences with some specific and important dynamics. This marginalizes the many residing outside the Box. To avoid doing this, we must identify and then remove anything that is holding us back from reaching more people. The two practical questions at this stage can help us do this. The first one is:

1. What is my Box?

A Box exists within our minds before it manifests itself within our methods. Therefore, it follows that our methods reflect the Box within our minds.

Occasionally, a Box comes in the form of an organizational structure, but more often in a mindset. Either way, the issue remains the same: Boxes stop us from getting ourselves invited. Therefore, the more Boxes we remove, the more people we can reach. So, at this step, we ask ourselves if we can see any Box in place that is already limiting the way we presently do mission, share our faith, or promote our vision.

For myself, when it came to reaching the young people in my hometown, all I really needed to do was ask, "Where are they?" The answer was clear. They were in the public school system. So our church identified our Friday night youth program as our Box. Then, they removed any restriction on me to only minister to our church youth group and resourced me to reach as many as possible whether they attended our church or not.

Jesus continued to remove Boxes in the minds of His disciples after His death and resurrection, even throwing Peter into a trance and giving him a vision.

> *Then a voice told him, "Get up, Peter. Kill and eat." "Surely not, Lord!" Peter replied. "I have never eaten anything impure or unclean." The voice spoke to him a second time, "Do not call anything impure that God has made clean."*[32]

Jesus did this in order to break Peter out of reaching a primarily Jewish audience, commanding him to spread the Gospel to the Gentiles. There are many reasons why a Box may exist; it might be the result of pure habit or the way in which we were taught to do whatever we are doing. Either way, Jesus wants His Church to spread and not decide in advance who will respond by allowing a Box to determine who can hear His glorious Gospel.

However, removing the Box is one thing; knowing what to replace it with is another!

Experience

The second question asked at this stage is equally simple:

> 2. What unique experience of the Kingdom can I offer?

Once we have removed a Box and opened up a whole new world of opportunities, we need to offer something that others do not! Bear in mind, if you are a Christian, you have experienced many unique things that the world has yet to experience. The basic pi lars of our Christian life are this way, including prayer, healing, faith, and so on. We *feel, do,* and *think* differently from the rest of the world. So do not worry that you do not have anything unique to offer. You do! It just might take a little thought and prayer to discover what those things are. Now might be a good time to reflect on that.

It took me a little while to realize that what I had to offer was simpler than I expected. The reason I got invited into schools was not because I could be of help; it was because I could offer help no other agency could provide: myself as a guinea pig on which to experiment!

Here is the process I went through . . .

It started with me taking note of other people's Boxes. You would be surprised to know how many places throughout the world I have been told that schools work won't work! I believe this is because the typical offer made by a church to a school is flawed. It is to present a curriculum, professional speaker, or program with a ready-made message that we believe the school needs. Then, when the faculty declines the opportunity to accept our proposal, depending on our denomination, we either go into politics or 'bind the devil.' Instead, I listened to the stories of the faculty in my local schools and noticed a pattern. They were not looking for better curriculum; they needed good role models. They loved the idea of young adults the teens could look up to, who would help the staff double down on the message they were promoting. So, I started to teach myself how to take a subject or issue the school was already dealing with and create faith-based ministry around it. After working on this idea, I visited the Manchester Town Hall where I asked the education department for their Personal and Social Education syllabus. Realizing that there were six parts of the curriculum in which I could be of service, I offered myself to teachers as a 'lab rat' using the following proposition:

> "When you teach law and order, you bring in the police, and when

you teach on health and safety, you request the help of the fire brigade. So, when you need someone to give examples of these six subjects—or any others you have to teach—would you like to invite me to help with those?"

Within a year, seventeen schools said yes.

When I arrived to help with my first class, the teacher introduced me to the students like this:

> "Students, if you remember, we are looking at the myths people believe in around the world. Well, last week we looked at Noah and the Ark, and this week we have found someone who actually believes it really happened! Let's give Mr. Gibbs a warm welcome."

I offered these experiences for free and on their turf. Doing so meant that I was often given 50 minutes to teach totally unchurched teenagers. I asked the staff to give me the facts they wanted me to present, but I taught them with the passion and creativity of a true believer. Usually within a few minutes, I would be asked questions on all manner of issues relating to Christianity. Within a couple of years, I was teaching multiple subjects relating to either my faith or Christian core values. This was mainly in Religious or Personal Life Education lessons but sometimes in other parts of the curriculum, such as the arts. I did this on an almost daily basis in those seventeen different schools around the Greater Manchester area.

Did you spot another key to *getting yourself invited?*

It is to build the unique experience on *joint objectives*.

You might say it this way:

> You will not be invited unless you serve them, and you will not serve them unless you help them fulfill their role, and you will not help them fulfill their role unless you know its purpose.

Learning these principles had a dramatic effect on how we train our youth workers. The Pais Movement does not give our apprentices a curriculum to present in a school; instead, we teach them how to create a unique lesson from scratch on joint objectives for any subject upon which they are invited to speak.

So what about you?

Your journey will be very different from mine. You have a different story, a different skill-set, a different situation, a different community to reach. You are also likely to have a different Box that limits you. The point of the template is not to tell you exactly what to do but to help you think how Jesus might do it. After all, Jesus taught us *how* to think not just *what* to think.

So, let me be your guide as you apply this first step to *your* world . . .

How?

Defaults

None of us can reach every person on the planet.

However, we can give everyone in our potential sphere of influence the opportunity to hear the Good News. Perhaps you are already thinking about someone you want to personally share your faith with or a particular group you want to reach, such as your work colleagues, local school, college, or neighborhood. In these 'How' chapters, we will revisit each step of the template in order to help you apply its questions to your personal relationships and wider vision. So let me remind you of the first step.

> Step 1 - 'Spread'
>
> The Principle: Spread and do not decide in advance who will respond.
>
> The Practice: Offer a unique experience of the Kingdom.
>
> The Questions:
>
> 1. What is my Box?
>
> 2. What unique experience of the Kingdom can I offer?

It may help you, from this point, to move forward with a particular situation in mind.

Question 1

> 1. What is my Box?

Boxes exist organizationally as well as personally. Today, as I write, I received the following email from my friend Dan, the national director of a UK youth organization and a Pais alumni:

> "Yesterday I did The Flow[33] discipleship method with a young person. We looked at how to make friends using the Shalom Strategy. When he suggested it, it made me laugh slightly but it was an amazing process for a young man who struggles to develop new relationships."[34]

This first question helps us identify the many Boxes that limit us even in our inter-personal relationships. It is important to note that, like the people who create them, Boxes come in all shapes and sizes. However, let me suggest one huge generic Box that exists in sharing our faith on a one-to-one basis, because it also hints at the problem we have on a larger scale:

> The need to first tell our story!

We might think the best way to reach our friends and families is to give our testimony to them in a particular fashion. But what if our story is much more effective when it is being *pulled* from us than when we *push* it onto them? And so, how might you get invited to share your message?

Well, it could be said that:

> You will not be invited to tell God's story until you first get invited to tell your story, and you will not get invited to tell your story until you first listen to their story.[35]

Although this statement is clearly hyperbolic, listening to a person's story will often lead them to ask you for yours. Plus, it will give you insight into the type of experience they may be willing to participate in—something *uniquely fitting* for them that you might not have thought of if you had simply launched into your own testimony from the start.

Listening to people will help you know which part of your story might help them most.

That principle is key to getting ourselves invited at both a micro and a macro level. Both may require that we remove the Box of our *pre-planned presentation* and learn how to partner with what God is already saying to those we hope to reach. After all, He started speaking to them well before we arrived on the scene!

To get what you want, you have to know what you have to give up to get it, and so, to find new ways of evangelism, you may have to imagine removing your default *modus operandi*. For instance, as a church, one idea might be to ask how you could reach people if you had no building or event to which you could invite people. Such a question may prompt you to think of new ways to get invited that otherwise may not have occurred to you. Again, this is how I approached schools. Removing my preconceived ideas of what would serve the school best, I instead listened to their story. I did not offer them everything I had to offer but instead I matched the *unique* part of our vision (providing role-models) to the *specific* need they expressed to me.

For those of you who have been on this road for a long time and have already found ways of reaching more people, can I offer one more thought based on my experience? Consider whether or not what was once your 'Box smasher' has now become your new Box. Sometimes it is hard to see a Box when you are looking from one perspective, so inviting others to help you think through these questions as a group can be beneficial.

As an organization, the Pais Movement's true calling is to make missionaries who make missionaries. For many years, we had limited that to schools. We knew how to serve the faculty and we felt comfortable doing it. However, as some of my friends are owners or CEOs of companies, they began asking me, "Could the Shalom Strategy apply to businesses?" The first company I was invited into was an advertising agency. Their CEO had noticed that Pais members, who were on the whole full-time unpaid millennial volunteers, had a greater work ethic than those the company employed. Therefore, he invited me to present coaching lessons to his managers, based on Christian principles, in the same way I had presented life lessons in schools. Initially, our uniquely better experience was the Biblical methods we used to inspire millennials. Since then, I have created other unique teaching series based on their questions and the answers we believe the Bible offers. The opportunities given me are the same as teaching in a school. Instead of a class of students, we teach coaching sessions to managers and employees. What had once been my 'Box-smasher' (going into schools) had been in danger of becoming a new Box. So, regularly reapplying the template has opened up new opportunities for us to reach even more people while staying firmly within our mandate.

What Jesus taught works . . . *everywhere*.

Question 2

Now ask the second question:

> 2. What unique experience of the Kingdom can I offer?

This should help you determine what you can give that is better than anything anyone outside of the faith can provide. Something that will lead them towards God. For Jesus, His preferred method was to provide healing. You may choose to do the same or perhaps your gifts, experience, or theology may lead you to other options. Essentially, you need to 'find your touch'!

My personal 'touch' is teaching. When I teach, people engage with the message of the Kingdom to a greater level than other methods I use. I have friends who are not Christians but will call me for advice knowing full well that I will reference Jesus in my answers without constantly trying to convert them. For instance, I have a friend who was responsible for a key element of communication in the new community where we planted a church. Within that voluntary role, she was receiving all sorts of unfair criticism from a minority of her neighbors and struggling to understand why people could be so hateful when all she was doing was trying to bring people together. Plus, she was wondering how to respond to it. Because my friend had witnessed the attacks I myself received using the same social media platform when sharing about the church, she wanted to chat. So, with our spouses, we met for curry and chatted through how Jesus responded to such critics. Then she came to church. Partly because a mutual friend invited her and partly because she told me that what I was teaching "was very different but made sense." She had tasted and seen that the Lord's advice is good and wanted access to more of it. Notice, however, that she did not experience it first in church but, instead, through the community's social media network. If she had not experienced it there, I don't believe she would have attended the church.

So, in what ways might you offer a unique experience of the Kingdom?

Here are three categories of possibilities.

A Feeling Experience:

How can people feel the presence and power of God, which is normally only experienced by those inside your Box, without first having to enter your Box?

The neighborhood we live in has an 'Artisans' Market,' so we began thinking through how we could use that to offer our neighbors an experience normally restricted to those who meet together on a Sunday. We decided upon 'Healing at the Market.' We put up banners offering prayer and healing for those visiting our booth. Whatever their need is, people can come to our stall and ask us to pray for them. I've also suggested setting up 'Prayer Posts' and hope to encourage our church members, who mainly reside in the area, to put these simple, discrete 'letter boxes' in their front gardens so people can anonymously post prayer requests as they pass by, knowing that the church will pray for them. It is just another way of giving the arrows outside of our church services a chance to experience what we get to experience when we meet.

A Doing Experience:

Have you ever asked why Jesus sent the disciples out in pairs?

If a person meets one Christian and is impressed with their character, they are likely to put it down to the persona of that particular individual. However, if they meet a group and notice the character of Christ as a common thread in all of them, they may realize that something greater than the individuals is at work. So how can you help people outside of your Box experience the characteristics of Christ's body by fellowshipping or working alongside you and your fellow Christians as you show love in your community?

A Thinking Experience:

Are there ways you can help people experience the wisdom of Christ outside of your Box?

Jesus came to give abundant life, not abundant religion. He taught about life principles, and what He taught works in all areas of life, not just in church. I have found that if people can experience one aspect of His Word making sense in one area of importance to them, the rest of His Word gains authority in the areas in which they have yet to apply it. This is the category of unique experiences that our schools and business outreach falls into, plus it's the kind that seemed to help my friend with the 'hate email' problem.

One final thought on this is that for years the Church has expressed the Kingdom's 'touch' through acts of kindness. However, I believe this attribute has become distinctively less Christian than it used to be. The Church has led the way in charitable acts to such an extent that secular society has adopted our ways. Now businesses are seen picking up the banner of various worthwhile causes, which is wonderful; and, of course, we as Christians should still take care of the sick, feed the homeless, and fight for the marginalized simply because God loves people! However, we need to ask how we can also evangelize in a way that is *distinctly Jesus*. Otherwise, we may be in danger of simply pointing people to our own self-righteousness rather than to Christ.

Of course, I cannot tell you what you should specifically do in your context. Instead, I am providing this template so that you can ask the Holy Spirit to guide you through it. I believe He will give you the direction and creativity you may need.

In summary, I have found that the first step to getting myself invited is to offer a taste of the Kingdom and avoid making assumptions of who will respond to the message or limit the way in which they can receive it.

Therefore, what comes next may seem a little paradoxical.

SPREAD

My Spread Strategy

Please take time to reflect here.

My Questions

Is there a place where more of the people I want to reach congregate or reside?

Do I know their story and their purpose?

What presumptions am I making about those I am trying to reach?

What is my Box?

What experience from inside my Box can I offer those outside of it?

What are the joint objectives it can build upon?

What makes it distinctive or better than what others are offering?

What problem does it answer that no one else can?

My Summary

SPOT

Spot the people of peace

Why?

Provoke

It seems to me that miracles are object lessons.

Signs and wonders reveal characteristics of the Kingdom of Heaven to those living on the earth. Therefore, how Jesus performed a miracle gives us insight into *how* He advanced the Kingdom of God. This is particularly true when understanding the principle behind the second step in the Shalom Template.

Many years ago, when reading the eighth chapter of the book of Matthew, something in the back to back stories of Christ's healing miracles jumped out to me. Up until that point, the Jesus I believed in was so compassionate that He healed whomever He saw in pain whenever He saw them hurting. His immense love caused Him to make the *first move*.

I was wrong.

As I reread the passage, I noticed that Jesus was almost always *responding* to someone who was asking for His help. He very rarely initiated any healing or miracle! His first move was not to heal; it was to 'Spread.' Jesus let people know why He was there and what He had to offer . . . but that was all. Only when others made a step towards Him did He react. I wondered if this principle went further than just the stories in the chapter I was reading, and so I stayed up until the very early hours of the morning looking at every healing miracle that Jesus performed in the Gospels.[36] What I discovered shocked me.

Out of more than thirty of Jesus's miracles, only five *appeared* to be initiated by Him!

As I cross-referenced stories,[37] I realized that in almost every situation, Jesus was *reacting* to someone who shouted out to Him,[38] reached out to touch Him,[39] asked for mercy,[40] begged for His help,[41] or ripped open a roof to get His attention.[42] Even when He restored the ear of the high priest's servant, He was being forced to respond to a mistake made by one of His disciples.[43]

Then I noticed that in four of the five cases where Jesus appeared to initiate healing, there was more to the story. For three of them, Jesus worked a wonder in response to questions regarding the Sabbath.[44] In other words, He healed people because He was being asked to prove a point. At first glance, the fourth case seemed to buck the trend. This was where He restored a sick man at the pool of Bethsaida. However, upon closer scrutiny of the context, I realized that it too lined up with the other miracles. The Jews believed that from time to time this particular pool would be stirred by an angel and that the first person to then get into it would be cured.[45] So, by going to that pool, the man was already crying out for God's help.

I could only find one case where Jesus clearly initiated healing! It was the time He saw the distress of the widow at Nain.[46] Here, without any known invitation, Jesus raised her son from the dead . . . but it was a standalone incident.[47]

In reality, all but one of Jesus's miracles were provoked by those leaning forward.

Jesus never brought completion to those who did not first respond to His message or His reputation. He never forced His salvation on anyone. He did not push Himself, His message, or its benefits onto those not interested in Him, His message, or His vision. In fact, as the rich young ruler came to find out, *He never chased anyone.*[48]

One particularly thought-provoking verse summarizes this principle:

> *Jesus withdrew from that place. Many followed him, and he healed all their sick.*[49]

The question that came to my mind when reading this was:

> *When did they get sick?*

Was this an account of the world's worst case of travel sickness? No, of course not. They were *already* sick . . . and Jesus left! However, when they pursued Him, He turned around and healed every single one of them![50]

Why is this so important?

Significantly, this approach also meant that He never attacked those moving away from Him, only criticizing those hypocrites who pretended to pursue righteousness when in fact their hearts were going in the opposite direction. This step is therefore crucial to bringing peace in a polarized world. Jesus understood that you cannot reap *shalom* by sowing hatred! Instead, He 'Spread' and then reacted to those who, by their words and actions, proved they were leaning towards Him.

Jesus was the most powerful passerby of all time.

Hospitality

To start connecting the dots between this and the template's second step, let's look at another 'superfluous' command Jesus included when He sent out the seventy:

> *"Do not take a purse or bag or sandals . . ."*[51]

Why was Jesus so keen for His disciples to rely upon those they met on their journey? After all, it was not an isolated or random request. In fact, in the earlier commissioning of the twelve, He went even further:

> *"Provide neither gold nor silver nor copper in your money belts, nor bag for your journey, nor two tunics, nor sandals, nor staffs; for a worker is worthy of his food."*[52]

The answer?

Christ wanted His disciples to stay with those offering hospitality for four specific reasons that were key to His mission strategy.

First, Jesus chose hospitality as a way of giving people an opportunity to lean forward.

This comes to light when we understand the etiquette behind *'hakhnasat oreḥim,'* a Hebrew phrase for hospitality, meaning *'the bringing in of guests.'* According to research at Baylor University, the protocol of Jewish hospitality in Biblical times meant that hosts were only allowed to ask guests about their identity *after* they had eaten a meal.[53] Although this guideline was presumably given to prevent the Jewish people from offering hospitality only to more prominent guests, there was an additional benefit. Those providing *hakhnasat oreḥim* would enthusiastically observe what their guests said and did, looking for clues to discover who they were and the purpose of their journey. Jesus therefore recognized *hakhnasat oreḥim* as an opportunity to spot those hungry to pull information from His messengers.

As an example, let's look at Christ's own use of the strategy. After He was resurrected, Jesus met two men on the Emmaus road who were discussing the events of Christ's death. He approached them, but they were unable to recognize Him.

Notice that He 'Spread' by getting them to share their story before He shared His:

> *He asked them, "What are you discussing together as you walk along?" They stood still, their faces downcast. One of them, named Cleopas, asked him, "Are you the only one visiting Jerusalem who does not know the things that have happened there in these days?"*[54]

Then, by posing another question, Jesus played dumb . . .

> *"What things?" he asked. "About Jesus of Nazareth," they replied. "He was a prophet, powerful in word and deed before God and all the people. The chief priests and our rulers handed him over to be sentenced to death, and they crucified him; but we had hoped that he was the one who was going to redeem Israel. And what is more, it is the third day since all this took place. In addition, some of our women amazed us. They went to the tomb early this morning but didn't find his body.*

> *They came and told us that they had seen a vision of angels, who said he was alive. Then some of our companions went to the tomb and found it just as the women had said, but they did not see Jesus."[55]*

Only after first listening to their confusion did He respond.

> *"How foolish you are, and how slow to believe all that the prophets have spoken! Did not the Messiah have to suffer these things and then enter his glory?" And beginning with Moses and all the Prophets, he explained to them what was said in all the Scriptures concerning himself.[56]*

Then, Jesus got just plain sneaky:

> *As they approached the village to which they were going, Jesus continued on as if he were going farther. But they urged him strongly, "Stay with us, for it is nearly evening; the day is almost over." So he went in to stay with them.[57]*

As they hosted Him, they watched Jesus closely, looking for hints of His identity and purpose!

> *Then their eyes were opened and they recognized him, and he disappeared from their sight. They asked each other, "Were not our hearts burning within us while he talked with us on the road and opened the Scriptures to us?"[58]*

The custom of hospitality was doing its job.

Now the second reason also becomes clear. Jesus always had the end in mind, and so we see an interesting principle begin to play out:

> *They got up and returned at once to Jerusalem . . . Then the two told what had happened on the way, and how Jesus was recognized by them when he broke the bread.[59]*

Those who are moving towards Christ tend to bring others with them!

Filter

Jesus encouraged the seventy to use *hakhnasat oreḥim* for a third reason. It had the same purpose as the miracles He performed and the parables He told . . .

It was a filtering system:

> "Parables compel listeners to discover truth, while at the same time concealing the truth from those too lazy or stubborn to see it."[60]

The idea of a filtering system may at first seem a little unsettling, but Jesus knew that both hospitality and healing offered people a defining moment in their lives. It created a point of decision where they had to make a choice and, in doing so, admit to themselves that they wanted to receive more of Him and His message. This is powerful spiritually, intellectually, and emotionally. It creates the kind of buy-in necessary for breakthrough.

Finally, the process of hospitality provides a fourth reason, a key to getting yourself invited . . .

You need to leave people wanting more!

The disciples were to 'Spread,' giving only a taste of the Kingdom of God and hinting towards an even greater experience of the Kingdom. All three tools—hospitality, healing, and parables—were prompts. They were not, in themselves, a fully rounded explanation or example of the Gospel. Instead, they were meant to draw out a hunger for more of the Kingdom of God.

Therefore, let me emphasize that this second step is not meant to deter people from finding Jesus, and we certainly do not dump people at this stage. We keep on serving and 'Spreading' to everyone. However, it does help us focus on those who seek what is in God's heart not just what is in His hands.

I once read of a famous Russian leader who attended Sunday School as a child. The students were fairly disruptive so the priest in the village of Kalinovka decided to reward any good behavior or results with confectionery.

Our young friend responded especially well to this treatment and recited the Scriptures with great gusto and piety. The priest noticed this young man and took him under his wing using various treats and rewards to induce great results from him. The young boy won prizes for memorizing and reciting Scripture 'parrot fashion,' including the four Gospels. He then grew up to become the leader of the atheistic Soviet Union. Nikita Khrushchev declared that God did not exist and began aggressively persecuting Christians, reducing the number of churches in his homeland by a third.[61]

Artificial rewards produce artificial results.

What?

Kerugma

The second step in the Shalom Template may feel counterintuitive:

>Spot the people of peace.

Essentially, Jesus put it this way:

>*"Whenever you enter someone's home, first say, 'May God's peace be on this house.' If those who live there are peaceful, the blessing will stand; if they are not, the blessing will return to you."*[62]

The content, or *kerugma*,[63] of the disciples' proclamation was designed to provoke a reaction. The message was 'Peace to this house' and it was intended to draw out those who were leaning forward. It was also intended to separate the wheat from the chaff in order to stop Jesus's followers from investing their time unwisely. This may sound odd, especially as I've just explained how important it is that we do not limit those who should hear the Gospel message. However, Jesus wanted to spot those willing to pull the message from Him, knowing that they were also the type to pull others towards Him. He needed a filter to create a defining moment in their lives and a way to leave them wanting more. So, what steps might we need to take in order to follow this principle?

Allow me to explain by first asking you a question about the following diagram:

>Do you notice anything odd about the arrows as they relate to the Box?

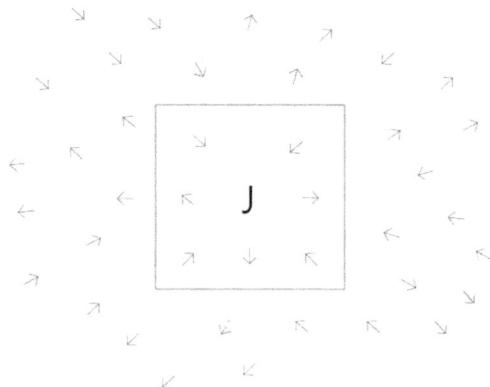

Not everyone inside it is moving toward Jesus.

Not everyone outside it is moving away from Him.

Using the analogy of a local church, people *within* a congregation may include both those who are seeking first His Kingdom and those who are not. Would you say this is true of your local fellowship? You will also notice that *outside* of the church, people are moving in both directions. In fact, in this diagram, there are more people outside of the Box seeking God than those already in it.

As we will see, noticing this can be vital to an effective mission strategy.

One of the reasons we can miss God moving in our lives is not because we do not know what a move of God looks like, but because we have decided what it looks like in advance. For this reason, we may be looking and investing in one area, but completely failing to see what God is doing in another. In the context of mission, we can be sowing into the people we hope will respond even when they do not, while failing to recognize and invest in the ones clearly attracted to the Gospel.

A striking and gut-wrenching example of this happened recently in one North American city. A public high school principal who had witnessed the impact of a Pais team on a different campus asked for a team to come and regularly minister to his students. Members of the faculty wrote a letter for us to pass onto any church that may be willing to host a Pais team. They were looking for a church to partner with them in this way so that the Pais team could serve in their high school on a daily basis. It was a real 'man of Macedonia'[64] cry for help. We then approached several local churches who were situated in the close vicinity. We sent them the letter from the staff requesting the church's help and asked to meet with the leadership to explain in more detail this incredible open door to reach an entire school.

None of the churches accepted the school's invitation. Most did not even reply.

Yet I can only imagine how often their congregations had prayed for the youth of their community. Sadly, our agendas and our programs blind us to His agenda and His possibilities. Not only do they limit how many people we reach out to (Spread), they may also keep us focused on people who are not interested in advancing His Kingdom while ignoring those who are. In a similar fashion, Jesus warned His disciples, saying:

> *"Do not give dogs what is sacred; do not throw your pearls to pigs. If you do, they may trample them under their feet, and turn and tear you to pieces."*[65]

To 'string pearls' was a Jewish idiom for teaching by threading Scripture verses together, one after another, to make a point. The disciples were being given strict instructions to not spend time sharing their message with those unwilling to listen. Instead, He encouraged them to spot those asking for a next step. We as individuals, churches, and organizations can also misdirect our efforts if all our time, energy, and resources are spent on the wrong people. I know that may sound harsh . . . You might even ask how spending time on anyone can be wrong! Yet Jesus clearly set this precedent as part of the commission, even to the point of telling His disciples: *"But when you enter a town and are not welcomed, go into its streets and say, 'Even the dust of your town we wipe from our feet as a warning to you.'"*[66] And so, the real question is not whether we should we spend more time on some than others. Instead, it is to ask:

> How did He decide on whom to focus most of His attention?

First of all, He did not focus it on people's labels, but on the orientation of their hearts.

It is too simplistic to say that Jesus loved only the 'sinners.' Nicodemus was a religious leader who sought out the Lord one evening, and Christ spent all night investing in Him.[67] It is too shallow to say He came only for the poor. Joanna, the wife of Chuza and a woman of great resources, was recruited by Jesus to become an essential part of His campaign team.[68] It is too superficial to say He hated everything the Pharisees stood for, because He told His own disciples to obey their teaching. Sadly, many of us can be *label-led*, and the vast majority of our investment is aimed at Box-insiders, those inside whatever our Box might be. Jesus, it seems, had a different idea:

He focused on those approaching Him, whether they were inside or outside the Box!

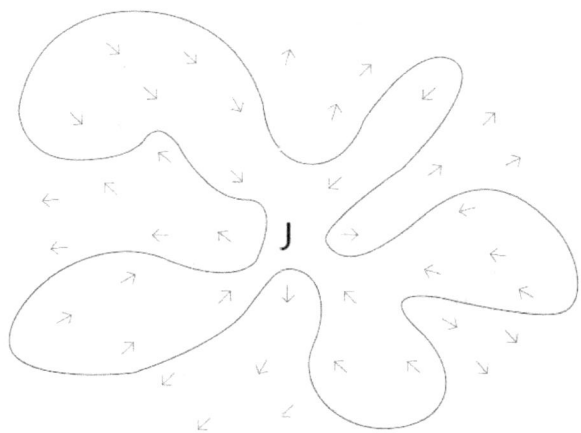

Christ demonstrated less interest in where people were and more interest in which way they were going. He never chased those moving away from Him, no matter how much He wanted them to be part of His Kingdom. Yes, He searched for the sheep that were lost, but He never hunted down those who were purposely walking away from Him.

At the Pais Movement, we aim to replicate His example. We lean in to those leaning forward, no matter where they are in relationship to the Box. We therefore spend as much time on those inside the church as we do on those outside of it. Partnering with local churches, we go into the community as missionaries while simultaneously acting as a catalyst within the church to make missionaries of those in the congregation.[69]

Yet how many leaders worry too much about keeping the few disinterested people within the church interested? How many put too much of their counseling efforts into keeping the unhappy happy?

Why do we do this when Jesus clearly spent His time coaching the most enthusiastic?

Christ had a plan for those who rejected His message (which we will discover in a later chapter) but He understood that forcing people to hear what they do not want to hear can do more harm than good. This was brought home to me even today when I noticed an eye-opening article from the BBC entitled 'Stop trying to heal me.'[70] In it the writer states:

> "Like many disabled people, I am often approached by Christians who want to pray for me to be healed. While they may be well-intentioned, these encounters often leave me feeling judged as faulty and in need of repair."

The report goes on to give some instances of mind-boggling insensitivity of Christians who, as the writer states, may be well-intentioned but have no understanding of how to get themselves invited. As a result, they polarize their victims' attitude towards God.

So, if the principle in this second step to bring *shalom* is:

> Spot the people of peace!

How do we spot them?

> We provide a next step to build upon the truth they already accept.

Let's examine what this practically looks like in its two parts.

Discover

Essentially, we want this second step to be a firm foundation for future steps.

If our goal is to make disciples who will make disciples, then we must give people a next move that is in line with Jesus's ultimate goal. We are searching for people who may later be interested in completing the whole journey. For instance, when Jesus first called Peter, He told him that He wanted to make him a 'fisher of men.' The next step He provided for Peter to take was when He asked him for the use of his boat.[71] Peter's positive response both confirmed that He knew Jesus was worth following and that He understood (to some extent) the ultimate purpose for which He was being called.

Unfortunately, we may sometimes be tempted to bait and switch, offering people selfish reasons to follow Christ but later challenging them to pursue a more altruistic path of discipleship. As it often has been said, we advertise Christianity like a luxury liner but when people get on board they suddenly realize they are on a battleship.

Jesus was an honest evangelist who preached a Gospel with the end in mind.

Therefore, we ask the following question:

3. What is the truth they already accept?

As I mentioned in the previous chapter, Jesus's filtering process highlighted an important characteristic of the people of peace. The Jews who welcomed the disciples were those who *already accepted* the authority of God's law implemented within Jewish custom.[72] These people offered hospitality because they believed that they were fulfilling a *mitzvah*, a commandment. It was a great way to spot those who already held a healthy respect for God's law, and it was something that could be built upon by showing them how Jesus was the fulfillment of it.

Paul also understood this principle and therefore spent most of his ministry focusing on the 'God-fearers,' Gentiles who acknowledged Yahweh but did not as yet know Jesus or understand their potential role in the Kingdom.[73] In fact, it is his stance in Athens that offers the classic collaborative model of this. Not attacking his listeners, he sought to bring *shalom* by building upon a truth they already believed in:

> *While Paul was waiting for them in Athens, he was greatly distressed to*

> *see that the city was full of idols . . . Paul then stood up in the meeting of the Areopagus and said: "People of Athens! I see that in every way you are very religious. For as I walked around and looked carefully at your objects of worship, I even found an altar with this inscription: to an unknown god. So you are ignorant of the very thing you worship—and this is what I am going to proclaim to you."*[74]

Paul, a Jew, could easily have been offended by the idols he saw. They would have been disgusting to him in the same way that they were detestable to his God. He may have felt well within his rights to lambast the people of Athens for their idolatry. This would, however, have had a polarizing effect, so he did not do so. Neither did he go on a social media rant or hold up a placard renouncing the sins of that generation. If highlighting his own righteousness was his purpose, that may have been appropriate. His goal, however, was to help the Athenians become righteous through the atonement of Christ. So instead, he built on what they already knew to be true, something they already understood . . . *that there was a God who was unknown to them.* Notice how he did this:

> He affirmed the little they knew,
> left them wanting more,
> and offered to fill in the gaps!

That is how you get yourself invited . . .

> *Now when they heard about the resurrection from the dead, some began to scoff, but others said, "We will hear you again about this."*[75]

If you think about it . . . isn't this similar to how most of us become believers? If I asked you why you believe that one day you will go to Heaven, how might you answer? *"Because the Bible is the Word of God"* or *"Because Jesus promised me."* In reality, it comes down to this: When you have put the parts of the Bible to the test in areas it can be tested, it has proven itself true. Therefore, when reading the rest of its pages, you believe it to be true in the places that you cannot, as yet, put to the test. This, it seems, is what happened to the father of a boy gripped by a demon. At some point, he had come to believe in Jesus as the Messiah but later said to Him . . .

"I do believe; help me overcome my unbelief!"[76]

The truth we have experienced can lead us to trust in the truth we have yet to experience.

Provision

Once we have discovered the truth they already accept, we ask:

    4. What next step will build upon it?

The people of peace are not passive, nor should we be. The fact that we are not to chase or force ourselves upon those walking away is not an excuse for apathy, a lack of compassion, or laziness. It is simply a call to direct our energy and creativity more fruitfully. To do this, Jesus provided people with a way to respond that was both in line with the part of His message they had already found to be true, and in line with His ultimate goal of recruiting them to His Kingdom work.

In the UK schools where I would 'Spread' the message in lessons and assemblies, the students' attendance was involuntary. They had to participate whether they were interested or not. So, in order to 'Spot' who might be leaning forward, I created lunchtime clubs that were optional. This had two advantages.

First, because students had to give up their recess time, I was able to recognize those who were keenest to pursue a truth they had accepted from the involuntary sessions.

Secondly, due to the voluntary nature of the clubs, school administrators allowed us to advertise outside activities and to answer a broader range of questions from the students, which, of course, led to more specific answers about our faith. All of this helped us move further towards our goal.

Again, we found that this practice of offering a next step from involuntary attendance to voluntary attendance was reproducible in many nations around the world. It built on joint objectives as teachers reported a reduction of bullying incidents at lunchtime, and, in most schools, the lunchtime groups grew in attendance. In one campus, we estimated that one in every five students attended the club and we had to turn people away when the venue became too full.

However, 'Spot' comes with a warning . . .

The people of peace are not always who you want them to be!

On another campus, a large percentage of students started attending a new weekly lunchtime club after a series of lessons and assemblies. The Christian schoolteacher I worked with had expected this to be predominantly filled with churched young people; however, unchurched teens and several Muslim students came along. So concerned was the teacher about these unexpected students that she decided we should change the time to an after-school program, hoping that, and I quote: "Only the more serious students will attend." She was right. The numbers dropped a little and the following week only the most devoted returned. All but two of them were Muslim!

Offering a strategic next step is a great idea, as long as you don't use it to determine what type of person you want to respond. The teacher's decision had indeed highlighted the people of peace. It was a group of Islamic teenage boys who acknowledged there was a God and were intrigued by the kind of relationship that I was presenting. I loved the opportunity, but sadly, due to unwarranted concerns of a potential backlash from parents, the teacher immediately shut down the club.

There are multiple ways of schmoozing. Fear drives many of them.

To practice 'Spotting,' we must engage with those who are chasing God, rather than chasing those we wish would pursue Him. Or, to say it more poetically:

> Do not cast aside the water you are carrying because you see a mirage.[77]

So, now let's take a look at how you might apply this process in your situation.

How?

Collaborative

How can you reproduce what Jesus did but in a very different cultural context?

To spot the people of peace, Jesus used hospitality but, since the dynamics of *hakhnasat orehim* are not a common practice today, how can we replicate His methodology? Well, before we start, let me point out that this second step has a palindrome-like quality. 'Spot' works both forwards and backwards. This stage can be used either to build upon a truth they have already discovered or to help them discover it in the first place. Both may happen simultaneously, so please keep this in mind as we proceed and note that all the steps can quite easily blend into each other.

To help you in your situation, here is the second part of the template:

> Step 2 - 'Spot'
>
> The Principle: Spot the people of peace.
>
> The Practice: Provide a next step.
>
> The Questions:
>
> 3. What is the truth they already accept?
>
> 4. What next step will build upon it?

Remember, God may have started speaking to your friends well before you showed up!

Through creation, which declares His wonder, and in many other ways, the Lord is trying to reveal Himself to those we reach. We are not introducing the presence of God to them. We are simply trying to help them connect the dots between what they know to be true and the God of truth. To bring *shalom*, we need to give them a next step that is *collaborative* rather than *combative*! The hope is that this next step will highlight those looking for what you are ultimately offering.

You are looking to provoke a response—not to polarize, but to partner.

Question 3

To begin to 'Spot,' you first need to ask:

>3. What is the truth they already accept?

I presented the Gospel around eight hundred times either on the streets of Manchester or in its schools before I preached regularly in a church. Therefore, I realized very quickly that there is a key difference between teaching Christians and reaching those who do not yet know Christ. If you try to take what a preacher does on a Sunday and make it fit in a workplace, school, or neighborhood group, you may be very disappointed with the results.

In church, the theory goes that if I can convince the congregation that the Bible says 'X,' then they will believe in 'X,' behave like 'X,' or become 'X.' Why? Because the Bible is authoritative to them. That foundational platform did not exist on the streets or in the schools of Manchester. Nor are you likely to find that it exists in those you are seeking to reach. For me, there was no point going into a classroom full of unchurched teenagers and presenting the need to do 'X' 'Y' or 'Z' because "the Bible says so." Instead, I had to do the following and I suggest you will need to do something similar:

>First, connect with a truth that they already believe in.

>Second, draw attention to it or, better yet, get them to draw attention to it.

>Third, build the credibility of the rest of the Bible or your message upon it.

For example, I would ask those in a voluntary lunchtime club to debate what they would do if they all crashed on a desert island and had to build a community. In every situation, the group would decide that they would need rules on the Island. So, during the lesson, I would give them time to develop ten such rules. Note that, at this point, I had not told them what I was about to teach them, in the same way Paul first highlighted their belief in an unknown God before he told them what he was about to proclaim to them.

When they shared their ten rules, I would write them on the *left* side of a white board. Then, I would take away the large sheet of paper covering the *right* side of the board which, as you may have guessed, hid the ten Biblical commandments. I would then ask *them* to point out how many of their rules were essentially a variation of God's laws. It was never less than six, was usually eight, and was even nine on one occasion. Building on this truth, I highlighted to them the fact that they instinctively knew that elements of the Bible were true and went on to ask them why they thought that might be the case. This led to some pretty amazing conversations, which in turn led to young people asking where they could go to find out more.

So, how might you follow this same process in your situation?

You will want to figure out why those who responded at the 'Spread' stage did so, and what encouraged them to do this. In other words, what was it about the experience you gave them that caused them to respond? This might be as simple as asking them the question if you are just applying this to a friend, although you may find another way to gather feedback if it is on a larger scale.

I would encourage you to allow the next question to be driven by the answer you receive.

Question 4

Once you have done this, move onto the following question:

>   4. What next step will build upon it?

People's questions can help you determine if they are leaning forward or not.

One of the Hebraic words for questions in the Bible is *sh'eilah*. In many places, it infers that the inquirer seeks knowledge as opposed to understanding. For example, "What time is it?" as opposed to "Why does time exist?" It can also imply that the questioner has little intention of listening to the answer and may only be asking the question to prove their own point or righteousness. This was possibly the case with the rich young ruler, who approached Jesus, asking:

> *"What must I do to inherit eternal life?"*[78]

Therefore, creating something people have to do can reveal their real intention.

> *"Go, sell everything you have and give to the poor, and you will have treasure in heaven. Then come, follow me."*[79]

In your 'Spotting,' if people have to proactively make a choice to go the next step, it creates that buy-in and defining moment that we talked about earlier. With that in mind, here are some ideas of next steps to offer. They are based upon the three categories previously mentioned.

A Feeling Next Step:

At the 'Spread' stage, you gave people an experience of the Kingdom. Now, at the 'Spot' stage, ask how they might take that experience to the next level. For instance, with those who invited you to pray for them and in doing so may have felt His presence, can you now create an opportunity for them to tag along with you as you pray for others?

Many years ago, we created such a possibility for high school students who were leaning forward. Our Pais apprentices and volunteers, who were ministering as part of a church outreach program, presented an optional next step for students to go with our leaders as they shared their faith in different ways in the community. One of my favorite examples of this was when Michael, a colleague of mine with a passion for intercessory prayer, reserved a community room in an apartment block to pray for any sick that wanted prayer. Residents of the community would gather in the room at a set time to receive prayer. The teenagers who joined his team were given opportunities to participate.

It was a great idea on four levels. First, it was a way to spot those who wanted more of the Kingdom. Secondly, it gave us insight into who was responding positively to teaching on the power of prayer. Thirdly, it led to great conversations when students would ask Michael questions, such as: "Why did this one get healed and that one not?" "Why did you respond that way to ridicule and this way to appreciation?" Finally, it required something of them . . . It took courage . . . something that all would-be followers of Christ need. It was a step in the right direction.

A Doing Next Step:

Previously, you exposed people to the character of the Kingdom by helping them experience people of the Kingdom at work or play. Perhaps now you can offer them the opportunity to commit to a more formal partnership.

In my community, the church I am helping to pioneer invited Pais to join us in reaching our neighbors. Churches that partner with Pais in this way place Pais apprentices with member families of their church who are keen to see a positive Christian influence in their world. Therefore, we offered this opportunity to the members of our small church and, while I was writing this book, something interesting happened. One of the church leaders and I are members of the community sailing committee, and, at a gathering with other sailors in our neighborhood, my friend asked if anyone might be interested in hosting a Pais apprentice. I was surprised he did this because, for the past 25 years, Pais host families have *always* been both Christians and members of the church. Yet he was going outside of that Box and I am so glad he did. A young couple immediately stepped forward to host, months before any church member did.

To be honest, this was both a surprise and a challenge to me. To my knowledge, Will and Cynthia were not professing Christians or attending any church at the time. So, when they offered, I was initially unsure what to do. Normally I would have declined their offer, but the problem was that I had just written the chapter on hospitality! Here I was writing about noticing arrows outside the Box aiming in and I almost missed ones in my own neighborhood! So, I thanked them both and we placed a Pais member with them. Since then, they have hosted two more. It has been wonderful to see my two friends partner with us. My hope is that they will be blessed as they continue to engage further with the church, and who knows where it might lead?

A Thinking Next Step:

Offering a next step where people can ask further questions is simple, yet quite profound. It is a key to the success of the wonderful Alpha Course that has been pioneered by Holy Trinity Church in Brompton, UK, and is spreading throughout the world.[80] It is the same reason that Haverim Bible Study groups are an ideal follow up to Alpha. Both have, at their core, an opportunity for those leaning forward to discover answers for themselves. Both allow people to *pull* the truth they are searching for rather than have it *pushed* upon them. Both require that people either opt into a group or invite you to facilitate a study where they are. Neither require people to be Christians to join, and yet both necessitate an intentional decision or desire to pursue a better understanding of God.

One obstacle to successful evangelism is that we sometimes expect people to know what their next step should be. Instead, we may need to provide them with a clear and tangible way of taking it. However, occasionally it might be appropriate to ask your potential person of peace if there is a next step they would like to suggest. Note that, if you offer more than one next step, the one they prefer to take may reveal even more clearly the specific truth or experience with which they have connected.

Whatever you decide, you might want to make sure that it is in fact a step and not a gigantic leap of faith . . . Remember, discipleship takes time and the smaller the next step, the more likely they are to take it. Remember, Jesus's first request of Peter was not to walk on water.

In summary, you want this next step to be something voluntary. It should be in line with the ultimate goal, and it may be best if it requires some kind of commitment on their part. Once they take that next step, it will help you understand what truth or experience has become important to them.

Once this skeleton of faith is built, it is time to put meat on the bones.

My Spot Strategy

Please take time to reflect here.

My Questions

Why did they respond to what I offered at the 'Spread' stage?

What encouraged them to do this?

Does my next step lead towards God's ultimate goal in their life?

Is what I plan to provide a simple next step or a giant leap?

Does it involve a way they have to proactively opt-in?

Is there is a next step they would like to suggest?

My Summary

SPOT

STAY

Stay and disciple
the people of peace

Why?

Asthma

Do you remember the first time you ever asked an awkward question about the Church?

For me, it was thirty years ago in the middle of an asthma attack. I had just taken part in a street theater production where I played 'man.' It was a powerful mime, designed with the purpose of evangelism and created by the organization with which I was volunteering in Glasgow. It took people from Creation to Christ's resurrection in less than ten minutes. Our belief was simple: we were going to change the world and it was going to start on the streets of Scotland. On this particular day, after we performed in the city center, I was given the opportunity to share my testimony with the onlooking crowd. I then had the privilege of leading one young man through the sinner's prayer—something that never ceases to be the greatest miracle of all. After doing this, I immediately turned to the leader of the mission and asked:

"What do we do now?"

I wondered how I was supposed to plug him into a local church. What was the plan to help him on his way towards growing and developing into someone who could pursue the Kingdom of God for himself? My mission leader replied:

"Nothing. We've done our job."

Instinctively, I knew something about this was wrong. I asked permission to take him to the nearest church I could find. Permission was granted but came with a warning: "You had better be quick; dinner is waiting for us and the coach leaves in twenty minutes with or without you." Briskly, we walked through the streets and upon finding a church, I knocked on its door. Over the next couple of minutes, I introduced the young man to the church minister and then ran back to find the team . . . but they had already left!

And so, my marathon began, a desperate and frantic race through downtown Glasgow to intercept a busload of my fellow missionaries. I had a stitch in my side and my asthma attack started. Then, just before I jumped in front of the coach as it motored down the city center thoroughfare, playing a near fatal game of 'chicken' with the driver, a random question came to my mind:

Do we really believe our vision will ever come to pass?

I don't think we did.

Our lack of strategy revealed this to me, even though we would stir each other up on a daily basis, imagining that revival would start as a small spark on the streets of Glasgow, burn from Scotland down through England, and eventually set Europe alight with the Gospel. In reality, we had no plan for discipling those we reached. We were more interested in our favorite form of ministry than in those whose lives we impacted. Our vision made us feel good, but it was never likely to happen. It was more of a dream to motivate us than something to truly work towards.

Yet Jesus did have a plan.

He had a strategy because He truly believed that His disciples would go on to make more disciples and eventually turn the world upside down. He adopted a discipleship mainframe whereby those He converted would spend time walking alongside the people of peace until they reached unity in the faith and in the knowledge of the Son of God and became mature, attaining to the whole measure of the fullness of Christ.[81] His commission went beyond simply filling a synagogue with people. He called His missionaries to make more missionaries.

He recognized the truth of the old adage:

> To fail to plan is to plan to fail.

Commitment

My time in Scotland was sweet and sour.

Yes, we saw people make a decision but we did not stay with those we converted long enough to integrate them into a local family of God. Therefore, we did not move them towards the next step of completion in the way things should be. We did not *stay* with them.

Before I unpack the third stage of Christ's plan, let me share four of its benefits.

Authenticity

A week after I became a Christian, God healed me of a skin disease. I would often tell that story in schools but with very different results. In standalone assemblies or lessons, it had little impact. Students were often curious, but many simply dismissed the story because I was a stranger telling them something very strange. They never knew if what I was telling them was true.

The lunchtime clubs had a different dynamic because they were attended each week by the same young people. The impact of this turned out to be far more profound than I first realized. After a few months, a relationship would be built and so, unlike an assembly or lesson where I was an occasional visitor, the students in the lunchtime clubs got to know me and I got to know them. In this setting, one of mutual commitment, my story became far more convincing. I remember one regular teenage attendee dramatically voicing his inner conflict during my retelling of the story by shouting:

> *"Stop! My head hurts! I don't believe in God but I do believe you!"*

The more time spent with me learning life lessons, the more the lessons of my life impacted him.

Engagement

'Staying' promotes osmosis.

People are more likely to engage in the journey toward Jesus when they can do it with you. The gradual process of unconscious assimilation of ideas, knowledge, and beliefs requires a conscious desire to engage in something together. It's like the caveats we used as kids when we were dared to do something by our friends: "I'll do it, if you do it!"

We see this when we look at what others have suggested are the 'ins' and 'outs' of evangelism. Reflecting on the difference between modernity and postmodernity, the following are said to mirror the growing need to change our methods. The first group highlighted below are 'outs,' practices that were fashionable in yesteryear but are now regarded as socially awkward. Below them are the methods we are told are in vogue today.

> Out: That which is presented as a sales pitch, as conquest, as warfare, as ultimatum, as threat, as proof, as argument, as entertainment, as show, as monologue.
>
> In: That which is presented as conversation, as friendship, as influence, as invitation, as companionship, as challenge, as opportunity, as a dance.[82]

Do you agree?

Let me first say that this black and white idea of 'in' and 'out' is highly generalized. Does Jesus's Gospel include ultimatum? Proof? Threat? Yes... of course it does! So, to say one list is 'out' and the other is 'in' is to throw the baby out with the bathwater. However, I do see a worthy principle when comparing these two lists:

The 'outs' are things you do *to* people; the 'ins' are things you do *with* people.

To disciple someone is to do something *with* someone, not *to* someone.

DNA

As a student, I had two teachers that taught me the six world faiths as part of my school's religious education syllabus. Both were Christians, and both taught the exact same curriculum. Yet, one turned me off God and one turned me onto Him!

The first was nominal in his faith; his lessons were all that I saw of him. He turned up to class, taught me Christianity and disappeared into the staff room. He had no connection with those of us who were interested in religion beyond what he was paid to do.

The second was fairly radical and believed in discipling the young men he reached, to the extent that he voluntarily set up a lunchtime 'Christian Union' where he would spend time with us. From there, Mr. Newberry would invite us to the church youth club with him on a Friday night. If more lads wanted to go than he could fit into his vehicle, he would stuff one of us into the trunk of his car! He was zealous . . . and yes, maybe a touch crazy! The youth club was more than just a series of teaching meetings; we would engage in activities together such as hikes, parties, games, etc. . . . and that meant sometimes doing those things with Mr. Newberry. So committed was he to these relationships that he was the teacher who indirectly led me to Jesus. In fact, I was led through the sinner's prayer by John, one of his converts.

Not surprisingly, it was his brand of Christianity that I caught!

You see, it is our passion that transfers, not our beliefs, and that takes time. It is the kind of Christianity we are most engaged with that is most likely to become the kind of Christianity we will adopt. To Mr. Newberry, following Jesus meant you had to disciple others. Hence, I disciple others.[83]

Without time spent on this kind of DNA transference, we may rarely see the other key blessing, a benefit so valuable, it will leave us wanting to make convert after convert and disciple after disciple . . .

Breakthrough

When I prayer-walked across England in the mid-1990s, I chose Wainwright's *Coast to Coast Walk* for my guide. The walk is supposed to take around 14 days. One companion book said that the moment of optimum failure, when most people give up, is on the third, fourth, or fifth day. "Get through day five and you will complete the trip." Sure enough, fresh from the city, badly equipped, and with little regular exercise, I set off from St. Bees Head on the West Coast of England and walked straight into the mountainous Lake District, the most strenuous part of the journey. Exhausted to the point of a mild emotional breakdown, I kept reminding myself of the advice. *"Just get past day five"* became my mantra. It worked. Once I made it to day six, the journey became much easier. I felt stronger and fitter and, after only 13 days of walking, I dipped my toes in the North Sea, happy and victorious!

Jesus was about to give His disciples similar advice. True breakthrough in people's lives comes when we stay with them. Sure, 'smash and grab' evangelism can lead people to say a short prayer and perhaps even a genuine conversion, but to really guide people into all God has created them to be, and all He wants to do through them (and you), takes time. In fact, while writing this book, I decided that I will do the walk again 25 years later. I hope to celebrate what God has done in the last quarter of a century and raise awareness of the cause in order to recruit more missionaries.

You see, winning people to Jesus is addicting!

But remember, you only reap if you are still around at harvest time!

What?

Kerux

The third step in the Shalom Template requires the most personal investment:

> Stay and disciple the people of peace.

Here, Jesus tackled what He obviously saw as a red flag. The command to not schmooze is a forerunner to this additional 'do not' instruction:

> *"Stay there, eating and drinking whatever they give you, for the worker deserves his wages. Do not move around from house to house."*[84]

Jesus believed His messengers, or *'kerux,'* would be tempted to abandon His strategy too early—not only as they struck up new acquaintances on the road, but also when they were invited to be guests in the home of a person of peace. He warned them because they might move along too quickly if they saw that another family could give them a better offer. After all, there would always be a nicer house to stay in with a more prestigious family and a higher level of resources. Added to that, perhaps those who first responded were not the 'pretty people' with whom they had hoped to spend time. Christ saw their weakness in advance and wanted to nip a potential problem in the bud because He knew that true, lasting breakthrough takes time. He was never a big fan of hired hands for this very reason.[85]

Even earlier in Christ's commission, through the means of a numerical association, He passed on this message to those He sent out. As I often like to remind people, there are no FYI's in the Bible. God's Word includes no superfluous material to fluff it out a little. Every detail has a purpose and the Word of God often uses something that may seem insignificant to emphasize something very important. For instance:

> *After this, the Lord appointed seventy other disciples and was about to send them ahead of him in pairs to every town and place that he intended to go.*[86]

The thought that pops into my head when reading this is:

> *Why did Jesus choose to send seventy disciples?*[87]

It did not take me long to realize that Jesus used this number to telegraph a message to His *kerux*. First, it is true to say that this number represented the table of nations, a reminder that the Great Commission is intended to include all of us. It is also true that it symbolized the number of elders that Moses appointed for a judicial system to the people of the Exodus, which was a forerunner of the primary purpose the figure was to convey:

> *Seventy was the number of members in the Sanhedrin . . . excluding the high priest.*[88]

Jesus's disciples would have been fully aware of Jerusalem's supreme court. Its role was to police and provide religious management to the people of God. Christ knew that moving forward, a different type of Sanhedrin would be required to disciple a different kind of movement and so, by choosing this number, Jesus was teaching the seventy that His commission was calling them into a role that went beyond simply converting people. Again, using a different form of *r'mez*, He was preparing them to spend time guiding and developing those they reached.[89] Unlike the old Sanhedrin, this new Sanhedrin would not simply manage the community, they would empower it. So, what Jesus's commissioning of seventy disciples tells us is this:

> To 'Stay' requires you to make a premeditated commitment!

We need to enter this step of the strategy knowing what we are getting ourselves into and being okay with that. Therefore, it is important to understand clearly what He actually meant when He said, *'Stay.'* The Greek word for 'Stay' used in our passage is translated many ways throughout the Bible, with the word 'abide' being the most popular. However, in this context, the most accurate translation is 'continue,' which is used elsewhere eleven times. Jesus wants us to stay with the people of peace in order to *continue* the work started in their lives. But what does it mean to 'continue'?

Importantly, in none of the translations does 'stay' mean 'stop'!

And yet, we often do.

We stop at teaching and rarely move onto training. In fact, some think that teaching and training are both the same. Teaching is easy; it just takes words. Many of us confine our evangelism to speeches, simply encouraging those we reach to attend more and more of our meetings and hear more and more of our words. Although Christ's disciples were given opportunity and training to *participate* in the advancement of the Kingdom, we prefer to limit ours to the classroom. Even the theologian Karl Barth noticed this, saying:

> "The Word became flesh and then through theologians it became words again."[90]

To 'continue' is to build precept upon precept or, you might also say, experience upon experience. It is to give those who are responding a multifaceted participation in the Gospel. Not only did the people of peace hear the wisdom of the disciples' teaching, they witnessed another facet of the Gospel ... its power. Likewise, our evangelism should combine both teaching and training, words and action, demonstrating and appraising, questions and answers, sacrifice and stickability. Essentially, we must *show* people what we mean by what we say!

So, if the principle of this third step is:

> Stay and disciple the people of peace.

How do we practice it?

> We continue with them by layering their experience.

Visually, that may look like this:

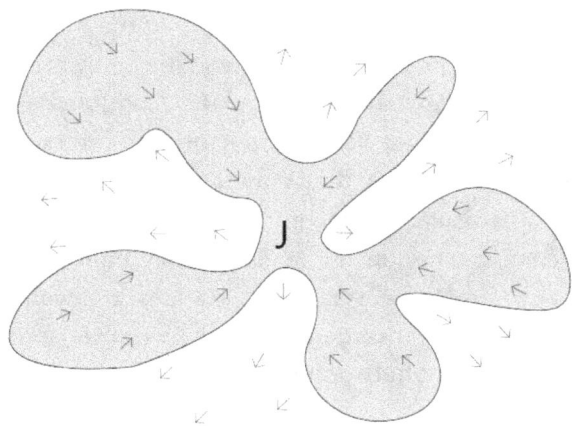

The shaded addition signifies the filling in of gaps, which is time given to layering people's initial experience with other aspects of the Gospel. Christ's example brings a new challenge. Although we put much of the responsibility on others to stay with us, usually by attending our church services, He emphasized our responsibility to 'stay' with them, requiring us to get ourselves *continually* invited into their lives. So what practices are required to get ourselves *continually* invited?

Well, we must adopt a *layered* not *linear* approach to mission.

Linear

To successfully practice 'Staying,' there are two questions to ask:

    5. What are the gaps in their understanding?

Once people think we have given them all there is to offer, they may cease to invite us in.

We have to therefore recognize and correct a common mistake. Too often we make our outreach linear. By that, I mean we direct people through a narrow, step-by-step, pre-ordained pathway into the Kingdom. We do this as churches, organizations, and individuals. For instance, as churches we may create a special event to reach non-Christians, which may be a good idea but becomes a poor one if a 'seeker-friendly service' is our only or even primary way of reaching people. This means that the friends, families, and colleagues of your congregations who attend may only ever hear one type of proclamation, rarely experiencing how the Kingdom can impact other areas of their lives. Once they have heard it, or even responded to a Gospel appeal at the end of a service, they may think that is all there is to it and move on. This is particularly highlighted in schools ministry. Students will not continue coming to a lunchtime club if they think they have learned all they need to learn. A linear approach decides in advance how people should connect with our message and offers few other options to expand on it. In addition, it only offers people a wider experience of the Kingdom *after* they attend church.

Yet, this was not Christ's example.

He filled in the gaps in their understanding, helping His disciples make a commitment to a full Gospel. Those He called knew what they were getting themselves into because, although Jesus did not soften what it meant to follow Him, He also took them on a journey where they saw God's provision, miracles, and breakthrough. Yes, they knew that following Jesus meant they would have to pick up their crosses, but they also experienced the power of God to help them do that. This gives longevity to a person's decision, protecting them from a hasty decision and a hasty reversal of their decision. After all, as the saying goes . . . easy in, easy out. So how did Jesus do this? The answer, though obvious, but may still surprise you . . .

To unpack His strategy, let me begin by asking:

When did the disciples first become Christians?[91]

Usually, people give me one of six different responses to this question, ranging from when the disciples first starting to follow Jesus all the way through to the Day of Pentecost. Some point to Peter's confession: *Simon Peter answered, "You are the Messiah, the Son of the living God."*[92] However, did Peter fully understand Jesus's role in the atonement at this point? Was Peter speaking for himself or was this understood by all the disciples?

Did Peter's confession meet all the criteria we would ask of someone we baptize? Are we certain he knew Jesus was divine at that moment?

His confession *may* be the strongest contender in answering my question, but the reality is . . . we don't really know!

Not for certain, and certainly not for every disciple. However, any discussions I have had on this subject tend to lead most people to the same conclusion: It was at some point well after they started to follow Jesus. The full truth of who Jesus is was still being revealed to them during their journey with Him.

So, let me ask you my follow-up question:

> When did Jesus first *disciple* the disciples?

We can all probably agree on that. When they first followed Him right? We can all point to the precise moment that the disciples followed Jesus and He started to disciple them. Yet it leaves us with a conundrum because, when we look at what Jesus did and what we do, there is a profound difference . . .

Jesus discipled people first, and afterwards they became 'Christians.'

So why don't we do that?

Don't we do just the opposite? We get them 'saved' and then *maybe* we start to disciple them. We must recognize instead that once a person has connected to the message via the power, character, intellect, or other aspects of the Kingdom, they may need a wider connection before they commit their lives to Christ. In fact, those who you disciple before they know the Lord are far more likely to go on the rest of the journey because they have a better understanding of what they are signing up for.

I will always remember the story of my good friend Pastor Derek Smith who demonstrated so well the art of discipling people of peace. Many years ago, he led a voluntary lunchtime club of public high school students interested in Christianity. One day the faculty decided to give every club on campus a special week of extended events, and so, a staff member approached

Derek, offering him the opportunity to invite the students to spend more time exploring Christianity. The staff member suggested a week-long Bible study. Instead, Derek made a counteroffer.

He asked if the school would allow him to take students to a neighboring school in order to run a series of assemblies on the subject of God's love. The teacher agreed and so Derek gave those attending his club a chance to 'go on mission' with him. Around 25 teenagers signed up, and only a handful of them were Christians. Can you imagine the conversations he had with those students as he delegated roles to them? Tasks such as "write a skit about God's love" and "share a story about God's love" led to responses such as, "But we don't know anything about God's love. Can you explain it to us?" They essentially invited Derek to unpack the Gospel to them. During that week, many of his fellow 'missionaries' became Christians as they experienced the Kingdom of Heaven touching the school they worked in for a week. Two decades later, several of them are now leaders in the church Derek pastors.[93]

It turns out that discipleship is the greatest form of evangelism!

Lateral

To move people forward, we need to move them sideward.

6. How can I broaden their experience?

A great mission strategy is closer to an album track than a hit single. A hit single is often instantly appealing with a simple catchy melody, but after you've heard it a few times it becomes very annoying. Remember *The Birdie Song* by The Tweets, otherwise known as *The Chicken Dance*? An album track can often have the opposite response. Some take a few plays until you really get into the melody. The music is layered with riffs so that when one thread becomes 'old,' you start noticing another. In this way, the track stays fresh. I still listen to albums I fell in love with in the 80s . . . They keep me coming back for more.

This concept is important in relationships, also.

In the same way an album track offers multiple threads to its music, Jesus engaged His disciples in multiple experiences. He sent them out with a catchy *kerusso*: 'The Kingdom of God has come near to you.' But He told them to 'Stay' and unpack it with those they were reaching. In this way, their message came not just through words, but with a demonstration of the Spirit's power.[94] When the people of peace had become fully engaged in one element of the Kingdom, they were encouraged to experience another.

At Pais, we tend to engage those we reach in one of three experiences:

As we 'Spread,' we offer the people we reach an opportunity to join one of our 'catalytic programs.' We have three major ones, including Because You're Loved, where they can get involved in showing love on mission; the Talmidim Flow, where they can be discipled as part of our mentoring programs; and Haverim Devotions, where we walk alongside them and facilitate their discovery of answers in the Bible. To be linear is to keep engaging people with just one of these experiences. To layer them is to create overlap with other types of experiences. For instance, if they first connect by inviting us to mentor them, we also work toward engaging them in mission and Bible study.

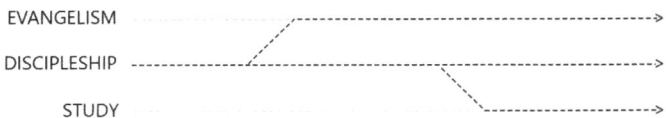

To 'Spot' is to provide a next step and, when they have taken it, we can 'Stay' with them, gradually broadening that experience of the Kingdom with other opportunities. Each new experience is a gift that further binds them to Christ and His message!

In New Zealand where we have some of our Pais teams, there is a helpful Māori concept known as '*Koha*.'[95] An example of reciprocity and a common feature of Māori tradition, *Koha* involves the giving of gifts by visitors to a host, or what we might call a person of peace. It is done in order to cement the relationship. A similar process is going on in Luke 10 when Jesus tells His disciples to give the gift of healing to any sick who welcome them into their homes. This idea of cementing a relationship inspires me because discipling a person of peace is like working with wet cement . . . That first impression you make lasts a long time and is hard to break.

Again, if the initial and primary experience of Christianity that someone receives is discipleship, then that is the kind of Christianity they will likely spread. Isn't that what you want . . . your disciples to go make more disciples?

It seems simple, but it works. In a world where young people are leaving the Church at an alarming rate and Christianity seems to have believed the lie that the education system is a no-go zone, we at Pais are seeing the reverse: youth groups are growing and schools are sending us letters asking for teams. But this is not happening because we are tweaking the existing methods of youth ministry! It is because we are fundamentally rethinking how to do it. We do not see youth ministry as a rescue operation but as a recruitment opportunity . . . and that changes everything!

More about that later.

For now, let's see how you can apply the principles of 'Stay' in your world.

How?

Before

What would it look like for you to disciple people *before* they fully believe?

Obviously, there is a red flag here. How can you involve people who are non-Christians in Kingdom work? After all, the Bible records instances of people attempting to do what Jesus did without previously making Jesus Lord of their lives. One instance was the episode of casting out a demon—and it backfired badly![96]

It is important to note, therefore, that discipling people before they fully follow Jesus does not mean we are saying they are already disciples of Jesus. I recently saw this succinctly stated:

> "A disciple is someone who has moved from being the *recipient* of the Church's mission to being *responsible* for the Church's mission."[97]

In our organization and in the churches I have helped lead, certain roles, positions, and responsibilities are not given to someone who has yet to make Jesus Lord of their life. Depending on your beliefs, conscience, and spiritual heritage, where you draw that line may be different, and I encourage you to pray through that. However, please understand that if you want to do what Jesus did and get the same results, you will want to disciple those you reach as you are reaching them.

So let me guide you through the third stage of the Shalom Template.

Step 3 - 'Stay'

The Principle: Stay and disciple the people of peace.

The Practice: Continue with them by layering their experience.

The Questions:

5. What are the gaps in their understanding?

6. How can I broaden their experience?

A companion to this book is *Talmidim: How to Disciple Anyone in Anything*. Delving into the rabbinic form of discipleship and how it relates to the learning cycle, *Talmidim* gives indepth, practical advice on everything from how to choose the right disciples to developing the various discipleship skills that Jesus demonstrated. I would recommend you read it. In this book, however, I am primarily explaining *where* discipleship fits into our overall evangelism strategy, discipleship being something that comes not at the end of the line but should be offered to those leaning forward.

So, let us look at those two questions again and get a little more practical.

Question 5

To prepare yourself, you can start by asking:

5. What are the gaps in their understanding?

Essentially, you need to ask a question that I cannot answer for you. What I *can* do is unpack that question a little more and give you some practical advice. As we have learned, discipleship is part of evangelism, not something you do after it. It is not linear, but rather it is a layering of experience. However, failing to realize that is not the only problem we have with our current understanding of discipleship. The way in which we disciple people can also hinder the process. Let me give you three questions that you might find helpful.

Is your discipleship too backwards?

In the book, *Talmidim*, I built a template for discipleship around a different 'Jesus Question.' It goes like this: *Why is it that we educate people and hope they have an experience, when Jesus took people on an experience and educated them along the way?* Have you done that? Is your idea of discipleship taking someone to a coffee shop, opening the Bible, and asking them a few awkward accountability questions? Discipleship is not about the numbers, but the process. If I step down from a stage where I teach a message to a thousand people and then take three people into a small room and teach them the same thing, it does not magically become discipleship! But many think it does. Have you also put the cart before the horse?

I do not preach experience *versus* education. I preach that experience opens up people to the education we want to bring them. In my mind, pushing our teaching on people unwilling to hear it is tantamount to scratching someone on their back. It is painful and unwanted. However, if a person has an itch that they cannot reach, then they might invite you to scratch their back and thank you for doing it.

Discipleship makes people itchy!

Is your discipleship too prescriptive?

In all three templates, *Haverim*, *Talmidim*, and *Shalom*, there are four stages. In all of them, the third stage is where we fill the gaps in people's understanding. It is where we build upon the truth they have experienced, the truth that caused them to become itchy to the point of curiosity. This is why the ability to provoke and then respond to a question, rather than execute a prescriptive monologue, is a skill vital to more effective evangelism . . .

> *And there was an Ethiopian, a eunuch, a court official of Candace, queen of the Ethiopians, who was in charge of all her treasure. He had come to Jerusalem to worship and was returning, seated in his chariot, and he was reading the prophet Isaiah. And the Spirit said to Philip, "Go over and join this chariot." So Philip ran to him and heard him reading Isaiah the prophet and asked, "Do you understand what you are reading?" And he said, "How can I, unless someone guides me?" And he invited Philip to come up and sit with him.*[98]

Philip did not show up and just start preaching a prepared sermon. He got himself invited and then, if you read on, he filled in the gaps in the Ethiopian's understanding, helping the man connect the dots between what he was reading and the personhood of Christ. This is the way to teach God's Word to those interested in Him. It always was and, in a post-modern world which values Experience, Participation, Images, and Connection, it is even more vital to overlap what our people of peace learn through one experience with other truths delivered by other experiences.[99]

But have you been trained to do that and do you train others to do it?

At Riverside Church in Exeter, UK, the leadership decided to plant a new church in a nearby city with an alternative to the normal service that their main campus provided. In this way, they sought to give a more varied experience to those they were already reaching. According to Pastor Aran Richardson:

> "We realized that people were looking for more than the contemporary services were offering at the time. We've found that people are looking for an authentic spiritual experience, the ability to participate and be engaged, whilst connecting with others in community. So, rather than delivering a one-sided 30-40 minute presentation where one person talks and everybody listens, we host a 60-minute engaging and focused conversation on a Biblical text, passage, or subject using the Haverim method. We've noticed that we are now developing disciples rather than entertaining spectators."[100]

At Riverside Church, Bible Study of a deeper form than most churches offer has been used in a missional setting to plant a church and reach the unchurched.

The path to the Kingdom is already narrow.[101] Let us not make it even narrower!

Is your discipleship unskilled?

Earlier in the book, I emphasized the need to get ourselves invited. Once we have done this, we will want to get Jesus invited into the conversation.

We are hoping for people to continually pull from us what we want to share with them rather than constantly forcing them to hear what we have to say. But how? At Pais, we train our teams how to do this in schools because, when a student asks a question, most educational systems around the world are happy for us to answer them fully. So here is the process we teach our apprentices:

1. Prepare the answers you hope to share.

2. Prompt the question with a hint.

3. Provide the space for them to ask the question.

For example, if I am in a school and I have been asked to speak on 'Making Good Choices,' I will prepare what the school wants me to teach and also what I would like to say about how the Bible helps me in my daily life decisions. But I will not say those secondary things unless invited to do so, always sticking to the promise I make to the school.[102] Instead, I might drop occasional hints during the lesson such as, "Actually there's a book I use that has taught me how to make great decisions, anyway . . ." or "I was once given a book many years ago that I have found to answer my biggest life questions, anyway . . ." In the lessons I taught, I would create Q&A sections throughout the presentation and quite often a student would ask me, "What was that book you mentioned and how did it help you?" I would then turn to the teacher and ask permission to share the answer as it would be a faith-based answer. In all the years that I worked in schools, I can only remember once that a teacher denied me that opportunity.

This is how I did it. It is how I still teach those leaning forward on a personal level. It is how I believe the Church needs to engage the world on a wider, more strategic scale. The principles of *preparing, prompting,* and *creating* can be used to get ourselves invited into the conversation. Generally, however, churches don't teach us how to do this stuff . . . and I really wish they would.

So, as you think through those three questions, what conclusion do you come to? How might your evangelism change on a one-to-one basis?

What might you need to do differently as a church or organization?

Question 6

The next question is:

> 6. How can I broaden their experience?

In the first step of the Shalom Strategy, you engaged people in a *Feeling* or *Doing* or *Thinking* element of the Kingdom. In the second step, you built upon that truth. Now, in this third step, you will want to create crossover. For instance, if you first reached them through a *Feeling* element, you now encourage them to engage with it by *Doing* or *Thinking*.

In his book on leadership, the legendary manager of Manchester United, Sir Alex Ferguson, refers to a *pipeline*—a clear system that he used to develop very young players. It was designed to help their parents see a long-term future at the club for their child. Pointing to the significance of not only having a vision statement and the infrastructure to make it happen, he writes that the infrastructure must be visible:

> "It makes it far tougher to sell the dream of the future if you cannot point to the staff and facilities that will make it come true."[103]

The greatest opportunities for mission come when people see us as a tour guide rather than a travel agent. A travel agent will pump tropical fragrances into their storefront office, giving you a taste of what may await you should you purchase one of their travel packages. They will open a glossy brochure and point you to its various pages depicting glamorous places with exciting action shots of people having fun. A travel agent will say something like:

> "You should go to Paris, I hear it's great. I can tell you what to do when you get there!"

A tour guide, however, gives you the opportunity to explore the place with them. They will walk slightly ahead of you, pointing out places of interest and telling you personal stories of what they have discovered. A tour guide will say something like:

> "Hey, I'm going to Paris! It's amazing! Want to join me? I'll show you around."

Rather than using the Bible as a travel brochure, we need to journey with people. We need to live out its pages alongside the people of peace, filling in the gaps in their understanding and provoking new questions. It requires your time and willingness to help them explore the Gospel by participating in it, rather than just presenting it. What you need to think about right now is this . . . Can people see that opportunity? Is that pipeline, as Ferguson would put it, clearly visible to them or do they think they are going to have to do this all by themselves? You may know that they do not . . . but do they? Sure, you may have told them that you are there for them, but it is far tougher to sell the dream of the future if you cannot point to the disciplers and experiences that can make it come true!

The challenge of the seventy can be daunting to those of us who are busy with life. It's a lot easier just to invite people to a meeting than offer to go on a journey with them, but let me remind you of two things. First, nothing is worth your investment as much as a sinner who needs to find his way home. And secondly, discipleship is meant to be a cooperative job.

> " . . . *the Lord appointed seventy other disciples and was about to send them ahead of him in pairs.*"[104]

Teamwork is the best way to disciple someone. Importantly, it helps share the load. It also means that other members can add their strengths to yours and offer varied opportunities to pursue the Kingdom.

So, let me encourage you not to fly solo!

In summary, whether someone is a fully committed follower of Christ or still searching to know if God is real, help them discover the gaps in their understanding, disciple them with layered experiences, and use questions to keep them coming back for more of you and your message.

Make your discipleship *simple* but not *shallow*.

My Stay Strategy

Please take time to reflect here.

My Questions

How can I disciple people before they fully commit to Jesus?

What is holding me back from discipling the people of peace now?

How can I overcome that obstacle?

Am I a one-trick pony?

What other experiences can I offer those still exploring faith?

How can I make it clear that I am willing to guide them through the process?

Who can come alongside me as I disciple others?

What gifts and opportunities can they add to my discipleship mix?

My Summary

STAY

SEND

Send them to
those who first said no

Why?

Rejects

One day a man was walking along a very long beach when he saw a young child attempting to rescue a million starfish stranded on the sand. As he watched, time after time, the little boy slowly and meticulously picked one up and threw it back into the sea. The man, frustrated with what he saw as a pointless exercise, asked the boy, "Why are you bothering? There are millions of starfish on this beach; you'll never be able to make a difference!" But as the child picked up another and tossed it back into the water, he replied, "No, but I can make a difference to this one!"

It's a story I have heard countless time and I've come to a very simple conclusion.

I do not like the starfish story.

There were millions of starfish dying on the beach, representing the millions who are dying without Christ. Now of course I understand the point of the starfish story. It is to encourage us that, when we feel overwhelmed by the need, we must still impact the lives of those we can. But my problem is this: I think the starfish story has become an excuse for failure. It essentially says: "As long as you are doing your bit, it's okay."

Well, it isn't!

There are millions of starfish on the beach . . . *Go buy yourself a tractor!*

There are millions dying without Christ and we alone cannot fulfill the need.

Even Jesus, although the perfect messenger, did not convert or reach everyone. This was partly because He focused His efforts on the lost sheep of Israel, but also because many ignored Him.[105] In one sense, I find that comforting. The fact that people reject my message does not necessarily mean I shared it poorly. After all, if Jesus 'failed' to reach some, then surely I am bound to do the same. However, it is the Father's desire that *none* may perish.[106] Although it may seem harsh to say that Jesus did not chase anyone, only investing in those leaning forward, He did have a plan for ones that got away . . .

> *He told them, "The harvest is plentiful, but the workers are few. Ask the Lord of the harvest, therefore, to send out workers into his harvest field."*[107]

Jesus recruited partners and sent them to reach those He had not reached.

We need to do the same—both as individuals and as churches. Just because your church may be growing does not mean that we, the Church, are succeeding . . . and to God that is what is more important. Just because your organization may be doing a great job at rescuing a few starfish does not mean that it is okay that many others are struggling to meet the need. We need a Kingdom mentality not a corporate mentality. We need to work together, sacrificing our individual status for God's greater good. As it's been said:

> "God can do great things through the person who does not care who gets the credit."[108]

Even as He sent His disciples, Jesus knew that the seventy would not be enough. It would take a second, third, fourth, and many more waves of disciples to fulfill His mission. He knew that they would not only reach those He could not reach but, remarkably, they would have more success with those who had rejected Him in the first place. And He was okay with that! Are you? Even now, the Father's heart never ceases to yearn for the lost, and so He challenges us to do even greater works than He did.

In turn, we must also acknowledge that our success is in our successors.

Parables

Have you ever wondered why the Apostle Paul never told parables?

In so many ways, Paul spread the message of the Kingdom just as Jesus did. He taught about the Kingdom, healed the sick, performed miracles, made disciples, and adhered to the Shalom Strategy as we will see later on. Yet I've noticed that the one thing Jesus did that Paul was never recorded doing was tell parables.

Why?

Here's my theory: People were Paul's parables!

Jesus used fictional stories to paint a picture of a movement that had not yet taken root. His apostle, however, was able to point directly to examples of the Kingdom expressed through the early Church. Paul referenced community members and others as examples of the Kingdom's work. Occasionally, he even used people to highlight what an attack against the Kingdom looked like.

The people we train are the signature of our life. I recognize my wife's signature. It is beautifully scripted and clear to read. She can recognize mine as well, although it is little more than an illegible scribble. When we leave an indelible mark on people, others recognize it.

> *When they saw the courage of Peter and John and realized that they were unschooled, ordinary men, they were astonished and they took note that these men had been with Jesus.*[109]

In fact, those we reach may become a greater example of our message than any sermon we can preach, for the following very good reasons:

Those you send may demonstrate the message better.

Those who are sent can demonstrate a change the Gospel made in their lives in a way that the first messenger cannot. If they are converts from a community you reached into and are therefore well known by the people in that place, they will have a visible 'before and after' story that the community can see. This can be incredibly impactful to those around them who have known them for some time.

> *A second time they summoned the man who had been blind. "Give glory to God by telling the truth," they said. "We know this man is a sinner." He replied, "Whether he is a sinner or not, I don't know. One thing I do know. I was blind but now I see!"*[110]

They are the proof of our presentation.

Those you send may relate it better.

They may be able to relate the message in a more relevant way than you did. They are likely to be native to the people who are being reached and can therefore use words and even actions more fitting for their environment. Like the woman from Samaria . . .

> *"Come, see a man who told me everything I ever did. Could this be the Messiah?"*[111]

. . . They may also have a better understanding of what is so extraordinary about your message that they will emphasize it to their friends, families, colleagues, and neighbors.

Those you send may live it better.

Another benefit is that those who go . . . grow!

This is brought to life visually by a simple study of the map of Israel. The Sea of Galilee is teaming with life, but the Dead Sea is just that . . . Lifeless. As Earth's lowest elevation at 430 meters below sea level, the Dead Sea is a final stop for the flow of rain and surface water, meaning water flows into it but doesn't flow out of it. Trapped there, the water evaporates, leaving the sea ten times saltier than the average ocean. In the past, the Jordan washed plants, fish, and algae into it. It was a death trap. The Sea of Galilee, however, is teeming with huge variations of fish. Why? Because the water that flows into it, also flows out of it!

When you 'Send' people, they grow much more quickly than those with whom you simply 'Stay.' They receive the message of life and they give it away. They become stronger in their own faith because, as the saying goes:

> To teach is to learn twice.[112]

Candles

In all of these benefits however, there is an *if* . . . a big one.

It will take more than just a willing heart for them to succeed. Early in my ministry, I prayed that God would put me in places and on platforms where I could make a huge difference. It was not long, however, before a series of incidents helped me realize I was praying for the wrong thing. In the early 1990s, I was unexpectedly asked to speak at a conference in Germany on the subject of schools ministry. Around that time, my work consisted of communicating profound concepts in a simple manner. In order to do this, I had developed object lessons to teach younger children. One of my favorites used 'magic' relighting candles. Do you know the ones I mean? You put them on a child's birthday cake and watch in amusement as the child blows them out, only for them to relight a second later. Giving various examples, I used these candles to talk about how God's love can never be extinguished. Anyway, I packed up my suitcase, filled it with my object lessons, and headed off to mainland Europe. When I arrived, I was hosted in a beautiful hotel and told that I would be speaking to around two hundred key youth pastors at an annual national assembly. This I already knew, but that night I also found out that I would be the only speaker at the conference. I felt so important . . . If only I knew how important.

Finally, here was my chance to make a difference! I was given an interpreter who, during the introduction of the conference leader, omitted the more boring details such as the health and safety procedures. During one of these quiet spells, the German Director said something of obvious significance and everybody in the room seemed to look at me surreptitiously out of the corner of their eyes. I just smiled politely, waited a few seconds, and then turned to my interpreter to quietly ask, "What did he just say?"

Her nonchalant reply stunned me.

"Oh, he just declared that everything we have tried in German youth work over the last ten years has failed, and that the Holy Spirit has told him that at this conference He is going to give us the new vision and direction for our nation's youth ministry."

It took a couple of seconds for that statement to sink in.

Then I remembered that I was the only speaker . . . and I had brought my magic candles!

Whether or not the Holy Spirit had indeed said this to him made little difference to the fact that two hundred influential leaders expected me to bring revolutionary philosophy and strategic thinking. Instead, all I had were a few simple gimmicks. Sadly, I was not ready for the opportunity and it passed me by. I had been praying for a moment when I should have been preparing for one.

I wonder how often this happens to us in our daily lives? I have found that most Christians are inspired to share their faith but may be ill-equipped to do so. They know how to invite people to a church event, but they are unsure how to get themselves invited into the conversation of faith . . . or what to do next. Occasionally, they can also miss the moment because they do not feel they are prepared to respond to it. The most debilitating fear of all is the fear of failure.

They have *tried* but have they been *trained*?

What?

Didasko

The fourth step in the Shalom Template brings a sense of fulfillment:

> Send them to those who rejected you in the first place.

The disciples were told to go to Jerusalem in order to reach those who had ignored Christ's offer of *shalom* the first time around.[113] Therefore, in Acts 2, we see Peter giving over 3,000 of them another opportunity to come into the Kingdom. Jesus knew His disciples would succeed, but how could He be so confident of this? It was because He had gone beyond *inspiring* them to *equipping* them. Those we send need more than inspiration. They also need the confidence of being well-equipped.

So, if the principle to this fourth step is:

> Send them to those who rejected you in the first place!

How do we make that happen?

> We equip them to reach anyone . . . anywhere.

We need to find new ways to train our people of peace so that they will 'Spread' the Word of God, not only to those who rejected us in the first place, but also to those we have yet to reach. Although we did not chase those who were moving away from Jesus when we first 'Spread' God's Word, the waves of missionaries we 'Send' may touch their hearts at a different time with perhaps different results! Visually, that may look something like this:

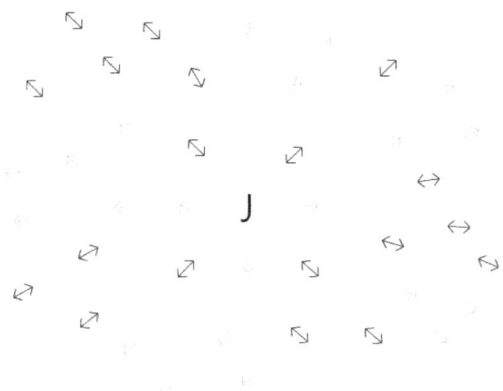

I believe Jesus equipped His disciples differently from the way we do it in two fundamental areas. Both require a shift in our paradigm. To introduce them, I want to point out the difference between preaching and teaching:

> *Jesus went throughout Galilee, teaching (didasko) in their synagogues, preaching (kerusso) the good news of the Kingdom.*[114]

Preaching, or *kerusso,* is different from teaching, or *didasko*.[115] To *kerusso* is to make a statement such as, 'Jesus is Lord.' To *didasko* is to then unpack that statement and demonstrate how it applies to someone's life or world. To reproduce Jesus's results, we must first rethink both our *kerusso* and our *didasko*.

Yes, you heard me correctly . . . *We need to update our Gospel message!*

Before you slam the book shut, let me explain. Contrary to the popular myth that 'our methods must change but our message must remain the same,' our methods have never changed without our message changing first. In the 1980s, the Gospel message I heard preached was "Turn or burn." It was simplistic and focused our efforts almost entirely on getting a non-believer to say the sinner's prayer. Over the years, the new mantra has become "Preach the Gospel at all times, using words if necessary."[116] This has led to a muted form of evangelism involving acts of kindness by an upcoming generation untrained, unable, and, in some cases, unconvinced of the need to lead someone through the sinner's prayer.

Did you know that in the US, according to the latest research, 94% of millennials and 97% of Gen X practicing Christians believe that 'the best thing that could ever happen to someone is for them to come to know Jesus.' However, 47% and 27%, respectively, believe 'it is wrong to share one's personal beliefs with someone of a different faith in hopes that they will one day share the same faith.'[117] This seems like a crazy mismatch. Of course, Christ's message involves both action and words, but what we have failed to communicate is this:

> Jesus did not come to simply *rescue* us.
>
> He came to *recruit* us!

He arrived on the planet with an invitation to join Him in the greatest mission ever undertaken and because of His death on the cross, we can take up that opportunity. Therefore, anyone who has submitted themselves to His Lordship has by default offered themselves up as a willing recruit to extend His Kingdom. So, in preparation to truly fulfill Christ's commission and continue His wave after wave movement, we must *recruit* the people of peace . . . not just *rescue* them. Yet this will not be achieved unless we share a Gospel that keeps that end in mind.

So, when I give the invitation of the Kingdom, it goes something like this:

> Have you ever asked the question, "Why do I exist?"
>
> The answer is actually quite simple. You exist because no one exactly like you ever existed before and God wanted someone exactly like you. You are loved because you were created to be loved.
>
> Of course, not everything about you is lovable, is it? We're all flawed and imperfect. In fact, we sometimes need saving from ourselves. Yet, when Jesus came to die on the cross, He did not come to simply rescue you, He came to recruit you. He came to invite you to spread His love. God says that the kind of religion that He desires is the kind that looks after orphans and widows in their distress and rejects the evil in the world that pollutes us.

If you are prepared to do that, to ask for forgiveness, turn from your sin, and follow Jesus, then He will fill you with His love so that you can bring that love to others. Do you have a sense of that already? A bigger reason to live than just you?

If so, can I ask you to return to the person He created you to be and live to advance His Kingdom?

This is the challenge I bring to those I am reaching from the very beginning: He came to recruit you, not just rescue you, and you have a unique part to play in His Kingdom. Then, we must redesign the way we unpack it. Now, you may be thinking, *"But our church both preaches and teaches. We even have equipping classes and courses, so what is the difference?"* Well, our *didasko* must change in two specific ways:

Incarnationally and *technologically*.

Incarnational

In the first of our two final steps, we ask:

7. Where can I first go with them?

Jesus's model was different. He *went with His disciples* and showed them how to do what He wanted them to do. His ministry was incarnational, not just instructional. Jesus sent His disciples to places He could not go with them . . . to the ends of the earth. Yet He only did this *after* He had demonstrated how to reach Jerusalem, Judea,[118] and even Samaria.[119] This leaves us to contemplate the following conundrum:

Why is it that Church leaders say: *"Bring them to me?"*

When Christ also said: *"Bring me to them?"*

Could the problem be that those we lead don't invite us into their world because we have never told them we are available? Or maybe they simply do not feel confident in our abilities? Perhaps it's because we were never trained ourselves? Of course, we want our congregations to bring their friends and family to hear us! But is the opportunity Jesus gave Zacchaeus available to them also? Tomorrow I will go to my friend's business in Dallas to teach on team-building. This afternoon I will work into my presentation a way to get myself invited to share my faith. If I am successful, I may get the chance to tell someone about Jesus and, just as importantly, help the Christians who work there see how they might do that themselves.

I learned the importance of first going with the people of peace many years ago. I saw how the benefits supersede that of more traditional ways to inspire others to evangelism. For instance, when I first became involved in outreach, I noticed there were two types of schools ministry being practiced that were less effective than the kind Jesus modeled. They clearly reflect the wider, traditional methods outside of just schools ministry and, interestingly, they are polar opposites.

The Professionals

This is where we hire a specialist to do the work of evangelism for us. Within the realm of schools outreach, that often means churches will send a team of heavily resourced professionals, such as a talented speaker, band, or celebrity. This brings value to the campus and builds goodwill among the faculty. Plus, they may be anointed evangelists whose presentation brings fruit. The problem comes when they leave, because the Christians in the school cannot duplicate what the professionals have done. The upshot is a short-lived Kingdom event. I'm pretty sure most Christians have experienced one of those.

The Off-site Pep Talk

The other extreme presents itself when students are taken off-campus to a Christian camp and inspired to reach their fellow students back home for Jesus. They may be inspired, given some simple ideas to implement, and then sent back to reach their school. The issue? When things didn't go how they were told they would go, and when they hit their first barrier, they have no one to show them what to do next. Essentially, this is what we do each Sunday with adults. We tell them what to do in their midweek environment but do not show them how to do it outside of a church setting.

Both of these methods have merit but are most useful as a supplement to Jesus's better way. I realized that this better way could be achieved when I first sent a team of average young adults into a local school to serve and share their faith there for a whole school year. In that scenario, the Christian students were not only given the opportunity to watch how it was done, they were given the opportunity to join in. The result is that the teens were trained on the job and in the field . . . just as Jesus did with His disciples. Soon we will look at examples of how you might apply this principle in your world, but for now let us understand the aim of 'Send.'

. . . It is to turn our people of peace into *partners* for peace.

Technology

Finally, we ask the last of our Shalom questions:

>8. What can I equip them with?

The second shift in our strategy is not that we need to equip, but that we need to equip differently.

For many church leaders, our main focus has been to grow our congregations. This has meant that most of our energy is spent providing Christians with tools to invite people rather than to get themselves invited. This is what needs to change.

Again, I am not saying we replace the former tools, but we need to prioritize this second type.

When I was younger, I was given tracts to share with those I met. These paper pamphlets were aimed at various audiences. There were tracts for atheists, alcoholics, Mormons, anarchists, materialists, and so forth. I used to carry them around in my pockets like a quiver of evangelistic arrows ready to dispatch the moment I met someone who looked like an appropriate target. As much as I feel this particular method is outdated, they afforded me a couple of valuable qualities that the modern church may have lost . . .

>A *responsibility* to reach everyone we can.
>A *confidence* to do it anywhere we can.

Being constantly challenged to pick up the tracts at church and use them made me very aware that following Jesus meant I should be looking to share my faith everywhere I went. I also felt equipped to give answers if I could get myself invited into a conversation . . . and so, I often did. Today, however, if we are given evangelistic pamphlets by our church, they usually pertain to a special event for us to invite people to, leading us to hand the responsibility over to our leaders.

We need tools that not only help us get invited but can also work in various situations in many different places. We need tools to reach anyone anywhere. Jesus did exactly that. He did not teach people a specific practice for one type of outreach. Instead, He gave a strategy for every situation.

So, how can you do that?

How?

Pivot

How can you multiply your success without multiplying your efforts?

In today's busy world, few of us have much more time to give, and most of us would love for the time we do give to be more fruitful. I certainly do, and I discovered a solution when I made a shift in the way I concentrated my efforts. I recommend you make the same shift in your efforts as well. Before I explain it, let me remind you of the template:

> Step 4 - 'Send'
>
> The Principle: Send them to those who first said no.
>
> The Practice: Equip them to reach anyone anywhere.
>
> The Questions:
>
> 7. Where can I first go with them?
>
> 8. What can I equip them with?

In 1988, I spent all my time trying to be the best youth evangelist I could be. I wanted to be interesting enough to listen to and insightful enough to answer every question persuasively; so, I directed my energy to honing my personal gifts over the next four years. Let's say I was quite good at evangelism—let's give me a 7 out of 10. Each year, I reached around 10,000 students but led a small number into the Kingdom and only a few were truly integrated into a local church.

Then, in early 1992, I read this . . .

> *When they had done so, they caught such a large number of fish that their nets began to break. So they signaled their partners in the other boat to come and help them, and they came and filled both boats so full that they began to sink.*[120]

If you were one of the disciples involved in this great catch, but you knew a week before that this was going to happen, what would you do? When that question popped into my mind, my answer was that I would spend the whole week building a bigger net.

So, I changed my tactic. I began honing my skills as a recruiter, inspiring others and showing them how to do what I did. Let's say I was reasonably good at this also—again, let's give me a 7 out of 10. Since then, multiple thousands have been trained and we have lost count of the numbers of young people who are now in church as a result of their ministry. Not only that, but many of those we have trained are now leading or in a key leadership role within their church. Some have even gone on to pioneer their own missional organizations. I pivoted from developing my *individual* skills to developing my *discipleship* skills.

The fourth step of the template encourages us to do the same.

Question 7

Of all the questions, number 7 may be the most challenging to fulfill:

7. Where can I first go with them?

In my neighborhood, the social media platform Nextdoor.com, which connects neighbors to each other, is huge. It has a much higher engagement rate than Facebook, and 77% of the households in our neighborhood are actively using it for everything from announcements regarding lost dogs to requests for plumbing recommendations and event organizing. My neighbors know I am a Christian. I can post messages about what I am doing in the community as an individual and also as a member of a church. Another Christian leader, David, often posts encouraging messages involving Scripture. The people in our church are mainly made up from the homes in our neighborhood and, since all posts are public, our church members often see conversations David and I have with their neighbors. Recently, a post about the church caused a bit of a stir, and I was able to demonstrate how to deal with criticism the way I believe Jesus would. It all turned out really well for us, particularly how it affected our congregation. Watching this apparently helped many of them think through how to deal with negative feedback they might get as they share their faith. As a result, they became more likely to do so.

As another example, last Christmas we purposely chose to put less effort into our carol service at church and instead used the social media platform to get our congregation invited to sing carols at people's homes. On the night the church met, the congregation came with the church leaders to a training party. Not everyone who came was a Christian. We trained them to sing the carols, gave them a cookie gift bag for each household they met, and equipped them with some simple tips for connecting with those for whom they sang. We then split into groups and sent them to the families and individuals that had requested a visit through Nextdoor.com. At each home, our group sang two carols, gave out the Christmas gift bags, and got ourselves invited by the families to pray for them and their homes. The church members watched the leaders ask people if we could pray for them and saw how we prayed. Some of the groups were invited into people's homes for drinks and conversation. In the days that followed, Nextdoor.com lit up with people thanking the church.

David and his wife Julie host a precursor to this where they invite neighbors to sing 'carols on the porch' each Christmas season. David shares his faith by introducing the theme of each Christmas hymn. About seventy people came out last time, a mixture of Christians and non-Christians. We not only identified potential people of peace, but our church members were emboldened by their leaders' courage and simplicity.

During the summer, we took the power of God to the local artisan market where we set up a booth offering prayer. The leaders led the way and some of our church members got involved. As we are still creating culture, most just swung by to watch us get ourselves invited to pray for people's circumstances or healing.

My friends Wayne and Terry run a successful business and create this opportunity through a 'culture of caring' within their company. They initiate workplace appropriate outreaches using the 'Because You're Loved' campaign and are involved in a lunchtime Haverim Bible study in the business where their colleagues can watch as they both learn and teach the Scriptures with others. In other words, those in their company who are leaning forward and are on board can watch their leaders do this within the day-to-day running of the business. Wayne and Terry's first tactic is not, "Come to church to see the message of Jesus explained"; it is, "Look around you!"

So, when can those you influence invite you into their world to share your faith among those they connect with? Do they even know that's an option?

There are three simple elements that you must include when you first go with them:

> It needs to be visible to your people of peace.
>
> It needs to be accessible to your people of peace.
>
> It doesn't need to be seen as successful by your people of peace!

It's important to note that people learn just as much from a person's mistakes as from their successes. In fact, watching us fumble through our new ideas, trying, failing, and readjusting, creates an atmosphere that encourages them to do the same.

If they see us do it, even imperfectly, they are more likely to give it a go themselves!

Question 8

In the final step, we ask:

> 8. What can I equip them with?

In preparation for this, please let me take you through three simple suggestions to encourage and equip your people of peace to go with you. Note that these suggestions grow in scale of importance, with the third being the most vital.

Rethink your language.

I do not *release* people; I *resource* them.

Can I suggest you do the same? Even to the point of using the same language that I have just used . . . It matters! I think the idea that we 'release' people into mission hurts our cause. When we *release* people, we not only infer that in some way we own them—and we do not; they are God's messengers not ours—but we may also unintentionally communicate that we have washed our hands of any responsibility. It also hinders our recognition of the need to equip them. Both present a 'sink or swim' opportunity to those we send out. And, that feeds one of the main reasons people do not join our cause—the fear that they cannot do what we are asking of them!

Rethink your offer.

Let me explain. When I was in school, several of my teachers were anti-Christian. One of them was a biology teacher who would often ridicule me for my faith. My fellow students would sometimes bring up my beliefs, hoping he would fly into one of his rants about religion and they could then just chat amongst themselves. One day, when the door of the classroom was locked and the corridors were filled with students from 'lower school' (our school was split into two buildings). He shouted at the top of his voice, "Oy, Christian! Go and get the key!!!" From that moment on, and for the rest of my schooling, every time I needed to venture into the lower school campus, the students would shout 'Christian!' at me in a mocking fashion. Eventually, it just became white noise.

Anyway, one day towards the end of my last year of high school education, my fellow students had thrown me under the bus again. My biology teacher was in full flow, switching between debating with me and simply making generic statements about Christianity, during which he announced that

Jesus was nothing special. I told him that the Bible said that Jesus was the only way to the Father. To my surprise, this completely stopped him in his tracks! I'm not sure why, but it seemed to really shock him. "No, it isn't!" he said. He actually looked worried, which took me back a little. "Yes it does, sir ... I promise you." What he said next brought the entire class to a standstill, and we all took in a collective gasp of breath ...

"Show me and I'll believe."

I could not take in what he had just said for a few seconds but then rapidly looked for the Scripture with every eye in the room upon me. Then, to my horror, I realized that I did not know exactly where it was. In full panic, I started turning the pages of the Gospels, hoping it would jump out to me. It didn't. After around thirty seconds, the rest of the class started to snicker, the teacher turned away with an "I told you so" ... and the moment was lost. I was crushed. After all those years, I had missed my opportunity. Like so many other Christians, I had been inspired to share my faith but not equipped to do it.

For many, this kind of incident becomes a reason not to share their faith in the future!

Just yesterday, a potential recruit for our Pais apprenticeship program came to visit me.[121] The person's only hesitation was that they felt they did not have the skills or experience to join us. Of course, they did not, but I have learned a vital lesson when it comes to enlisting others—one of the best recruiting tools we have is to *offer training* as part of our recruitment drive. Rather than inspiring them with words like, "You can do this!", I tell them, "We can do this!"

Here is a typical line I use:

> "We need you to do this. Right now, you can't do it. But here is how we will train you on the job ..."

I then unpack whatever training we have in mind for them.

Trust me ... It helps!

Rethink your tools.

The vast majority of people are average. You therefore need tools that the average person can use to get themselves invited. Otherwise, they will simply try to bring those they want to reach to hear you. If you want to build a church congregation, that alone may be fine. If you want to advance the Kingdom of God . . . it's not. In the church my wife and I recently helped plant, the tagline I proposed was *'To equip the saints for works of service.'* We are attempting a culture-shift whereby church members do not view the leaders as those who do the work for them, but as those appointed to equip them to do it for themselves. As I have already said, those who feel they are equipped will be more likely to take up the challenge. Therefore, over recent years, my strategy has been to provide templates.[122] I've found that these mobilize, as well as help people, due to the following qualities:

> They are generic and can be adapted in various situations.
>
> They have just a few simple stages driven by specific questions.
>
> They do not involve any skills that the average person does not have.

My hope is that the wider Church will work with their partners on templates of their own. As an example, however, let me share some of the key ones that I use to equip people:

> *For Discipleship:* To help others reproduce what God has done in and through them, we use the Talmidim Flow which employs the following four steps: Experience It, Question It, Understand It, and Multiply It.
>
> *For Bible Study:* To provide a new way of helping Christians use the Bible to share their faith with their friends, the Haverim Devotions method uses a rabbinic process with the following four levels: Context, Connections, Collaboration, and Contemplation.
>
> *For Evangelism:* Using this book's Shalom Template, the 'Because You're Loved' program gives people an opportunity to be trained in how to show, share, and bring others to faith. You can find out more about BYL in the appendix.

The point of these templates is that they do not just teach people *what* to think but *how* to think. They are more about an adaptable strategy than a rigid structure. In other words, once someone has been given a little training in how to use a template, they can use it with anyone in any situation.

So, how can you multiply your success without multiplying your efforts?

> *"Still other seed fell on good soil. It came up, grew and produced a crop, some multiplying thirty, some sixty, some a hundred times."*[123]

The people of peace are the good soil, so sink your time into them. Show them how to do what you just did. In this way, the message will be reproduced time and again. In all of this, never stop 'Spreading' because it is the platform the other steps are built upon. The more people you reach, the greater the number of people of peace you will discover. The more of them you have, the choosier you can be as to whom you disciple. The better the quality of discipleship, the more likely they will do greater things and reach more people than you ever could.

This is the strategy Jesus gave His disciples . . . but where else do we see it?

My Send Strategy

Please take time to reflect here.

My Questions

Where can I go to show people how to do what they must do?

How can I let them know I am willing to first go with them?

Where can they invite me into their world?

What tools can I give my people of peace to share their faith?

Would those tools work in a variety of situations?

Can the average person reproduce what I have done?

My Summary

Strategy

Application

Was the strategy of Mark 10 and Luke 10 just a one-off commission?

Or, was it specifically designed for the disciples of Jesus in the particular neighborhoods where He was sending them?

Was it reproduced by others? Well, I'm glad you asked!

As you would expect, years later we see it replicated by Paul the Apostle. Here, the great pioneer demonstrates how to take the template Christ laid down and successfully apply it in a very different situation than the ones Jesus or His disciples had faced.

> *During the night Paul had a vision of a man of Macedonia standing and begging him, "Come over to Macedonia and help us." After Paul had seen the vision, we got ready at once to leave for Macedonia, concluding that God had called us to preach the Gospel to them.*[124]

Philippi, a city in Macedonia, differed in many ways from areas he had previously evangelized. The people were not Jews and had a different primary language. It was a Roman colony full of veterans who were not anti-Rome as most of the Jews were. In fact, they were proud to be part of it!

Above all of these obstacles, one was particularly significant . . .

There were no synagogues!

Normally, Paul would use his credentials to get invited into the synagogues to preach. In Philippi, however, that option was not available to him. Here, the Jewish religion was not legal and therefore had no official place within the city where he might find the usual prospects to whom he would proclaim Jesus. So, Paul puts the Shalom Strategy into effect . . .

First, he 'Spreads':

> *On the Sabbath we went outside the city gate to the river, where we expected to find a place of prayer.*[125]

To publicly preach, Paul had to be outside the sacred boundary of the city because of Judaism's lack of legal standing there. He also knew that any Jews or God-fearers would gather near a flowing river, as water was crucial for ceremonial cleansing and therefore worship. Following Jesus's example, Paul did not force himself on anyone but instead offered himself as a teacher to those who might want teaching:

> *We sat down and began to speak to the women who had gathered there.*[126]

To sit was a sign that he wanted to teach, essentially getting himself invited into the conversation.

Secondly, he 'Spots':

> *One of those listening was a woman named Lydia, a dealer in purple cloth from the city of Thyatira, who was a worshipper of God. The Lord opened her heart to respond to Paul's message.*[127]

Paul had not decided in advance who he wanted to respond, so he noticed that Lydia was the first person to open her home to him.

> *When she and the members of her household were baptized, she invited us to her home. "If you consider me a believer in the Lord," she said, "come and stay at my house."*[128]

As Jesus had done and as the disciples had been commanded to do, we see Paul discovering who to invest in via the dynamic of *hakhnasat oreḥim*, the 'bringing in of guests.'

He then 'Stays':

> *And she persuaded us.*[129]

This infers that Paul, like Jesus, had played a little hard to get. However, he of course did stay with Lydia, and history demonstrates that he clearly discipled her and her household, layering them with the various teaching and experiences of the Christian faith. Why is this clear? Because he could then take them through the fourth step . . .

Finally, he 'Sends':

> *After Paul and Silas came out of the prison, they went to Lydia's house, where they met with the brothers and sisters and encouraged them.*[130]

Later in Paul's mission, Lydia had become an active member of the church and was reaching out to her own community. The people filling that room would have been those who may not have responded to Paul's first outreach. Lydia, just like Peter, converted her home into a church where the saints gathered to worship God. According to excavators, in the years immediately following Jesus's death, the function of Peter's home changed dramatically. The main room was altered and completely plastered over from floor to ceiling. The pottery it contained, previously household cooking pots and bowls, became large storage jars and oil lamps. Such radical alterations indicate that the house no longer functioned as a residence but instead had become a place for communal gatherings similar to Lydia's home. Later, the plastered room from the original house was renovated into the central hall of a rudimentary church. Archeologists have revealed that more than a hundred graffiti illustrations were scratched into its walls including crosses, pictures of boats and statements written in Greek, Syriac, or Hebrew such as: "Lord Jesus Christ, help thy servant" or "Christ have mercy."

Jesus sent Peter, and Paul sent Lydia, to reach those not yet reached.

Two thousand years later, we also emphasize the need to remodel our church buildings to make them relevant places to reach the lost. This, in my opinion, is a good thing. After all, how can we train people if we cannot attract them? However, the disproportionate effort put into making our services attractive contrasts starkly with the amount of resources we give our congregations to reach the lost. This has led to a very real problem.

I am not the only one who has had church leaders say to me:

> "Paul, I have built a crowd, but I am not sure I have built disciples."

These same leaders have also shared a further frustration:

> "I really want to go beyond attraction and assimilation to equipping and sending, but every time I go to a conference, I am given tools to do the first but not the second."

It is my conviction that this needs to be the next big movement in the Church, equipping those we have attracted with new tools to make more disciples. It seems to me that Paul had the same idea when he wrote:

> "... *pattern your lives after mine, and learn from those who follow our example.*"[131]

Paul adopted the Shalom Strategy and I pray that you will do the same. I hope this book has provoked you and given you the encouragement you need. We can do this! The Church has reinvented its structures many times, striving to fulfill what Christ envisioned it to be. We can do it again, if we are prepared to open our hearts to new concepts and get our hands on new tools.

I hope that this book can be part of that journey.

The Shalom Strategy can be used in individual evangelism, organized mission, and any vision that hopes to recruit, engage, and involve others. It can be used by anyone with the right motive, to reach anyone with the right heart, in any place throughout the world. At its core is the idea that we can reach the Roberts of the world, the lost and given up on . . . but only if we seek to ask a different kind of question:

> *How do we get ourselves invited?*

SOURCES

#shalom

SHALOM TEMPLATE

Step 1 - Spread

The Principle: Spread and do not decide in advance who will respond.
The Practice: Offer a unique experience of the Kingdom.

The Questions:
1. What is my Box?
2. What unique experience of the Kingdom can I offer?

Step 2 - Spot

The Principle: Spot the people of peace.
The Practice: Provide a next step.

The Questions:
3. What is the truth they already accept?
4. What next step will build upon it?

Step 3 - Stay

The Principle: Stay and disciple the people of peace.
The Practice: Continue with them by layering their experience.

The Questions:
5. What are the gaps in their understanding?
6. How can I broaden their experience?

Step 4 - Send

The Principle: Send them to those who first said no.
The Practice: Equip them to reach anyone, anywhere.

The Questions:
7. Where can I first go with them?
8. What can I equip them with?

SHALOM TEMPLATE

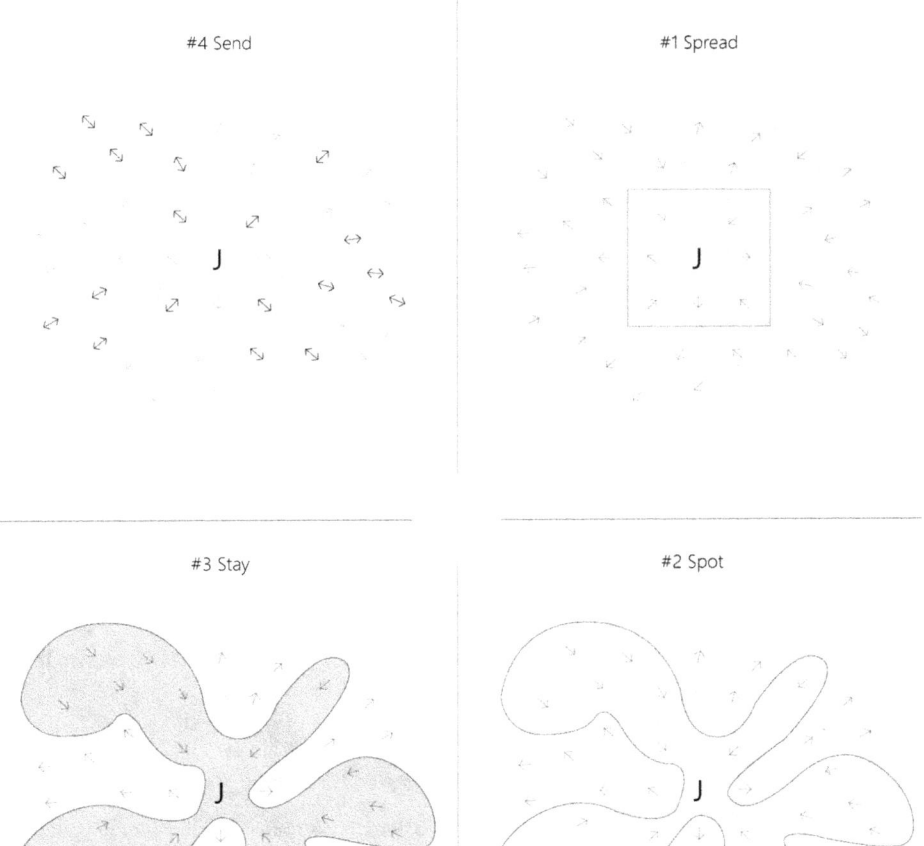

Copyright © Paul Clayton Gibbs 2011

Endnotes

1. Manchester City Council Housing Publication 03.01.01, January 2003.

2. Luke 19:5-6.

3. You can view the Charter of Conduct at https://paismovement.com/wp-content/uploads/2018/07/Charter-of-Conduct.pdf.

4. The disclaimer was something like: "I am an invited guest of the school and what I say in this lesson may not reflect the stance of the school. I am here as an external example for you to question."

5. This refers to *Kingdom Pioneering* (Harris House Publishing: 2017), where I described Oneighty, the 7th – 12th grade ministry of Church on the Move in Tulsa, Oklahoma.

6. Ephesians 4:11-12, abbreviated.

7. Matthew 10:34; also, note that the Greek word for peace used here is not *shalom* but Strong's G1515: *eirēnē*.

8. Cornelius Plantinga, *Not the Way It's Supposed to Be* (Grand Rapids, MI: Eerdmans, 1999), p. 10.

9. Later we will examine an example of this found in Acts 16.

10. I will refer to the other two later in this book, but they are Mark 6:7-13, Matthew 10:6-15, and Luke 9:1-6.

11. Luke 10:1-11. This is a compilation of NLV and NIV translations and is abridged.

12. POP stands for People of Peace. I saw something similar to a simpler version of my POP Chart when I first came into ministry 30 years ago, but I cannot remember or find the source. I have been told similar diagrams exist, but unable to locate any, I have created this to make it readily available for you.

13. Luke 10:4.

14. Mishnah Berakhot 5.1 quoted in the book *Meet the Rabbis* by Brad Young.

15. For more on the concept of intention from a Jewish perspective see the mini-chapter Kavanah on page 99 of the book *Talmidim: How to Disciple Anyone in Anything* (Colleyville, TX: Harris House Publishing, 2016).

16. *Jewish New Testament Commentary* (Lederer Messianic Publications, 1992) regarding Luke 10:4.

17. This was mandated as part of the 1988 Education Act as detailed in the book *The Thatcher Revolution: Margaret Thatcher, John Major, Tony Blair, and the Transformation of Modern Britain, 1979-2001 / Edition 1* by Earl A. Reitan. It was based on a rule introduced in 1944 and was also later formalized to a greater degree in 1994.

18. In the UK, homeschooling and alternative forms of education were very rare in the 1980s and are still relatively uncommon today.

SOURCES

19. Peter Brierley, UK Church Statistics 2, 2010–2020 (Tonbridge: ADBC Publishers, 2014).

20. See Mark 10:37 and Luke 9:46.

21. My paraphrase of John 3:30.

22. Luke 10:7.

23. Luke 10:17-20 NKJV.

24. Haverim Devotions™ is a method of Bible study I developed based on rabbinic study methods from the Second Temple period. To understand how Jesus was referencing Isaiah, you may need to research the four levels of Bible Study used by the rabbis. They are outlined in another book in this series, *Haverim: How to Study Anything with Anyone* (Colleyville, TX: Harris House Publishing, 2017). The explanation of the second level, *r'mez*, is found on pp. 48-61.

25. Isaiah 11:8 NIV 1984.

26. This was explained to me by Pastor David Shearman during a Pastoral Training day.

27. Andrew Ellson, 'Luxury brands including Burberry burn stock worth millions,' *The Times* (July 19, 2018). https://www.thetimes.co.uk/article/luxury-brands-burning-stock-worth-millions-zxxscjcmj

28. Luke 10:1 NLT.

29. You can read about this story in the Book of Jonah but especially in Jonah 1:2-4.

30. Strong's #2784: *kerusso* (pronounced kay-roos'-so), meaning "to be a herald, proclaim."

31. Luke 10:9.

32. Acts 10:13-15.

33. The Flow is a discipleship template I wrote about in *Talmidim: How to Disciple Anyone Anywhere* (Colleyville, TX: Harris House Publishing, 2016).

34. Edited for cohesion.

35. Thank you to Kevin Pimblott who gave me the seed of that thought in a conversation about personal evangelism.

36. This is based on a list of the miracles of Jesus in *The NIV Study Bible*, plus others I found.

37. Note that some Gospel accounts do not mention a request by the recipient of a miracle whereas the same story in another Gospel account records it.

38. Mark 10:47.

39. Matthew 9:20–22.

40. Mark 5:1-20 - This is clear as Jesus responded to the man/demons within him and cast them out. However, it says Jesus had previously told the demons to come out. This, it seems, was in response to the man initially coming to meet Jesus in verse 2 with the intention of looking for help as implied by his reaction in verse 19.

41. Matthew 15:21-28.

42. Mark 2:4.

43. Luke 22:49-51 - Thanks to Ryan Rodriguez for reminding me of this instance. Note that a rabbi was responsible for the actions of their disciple.

44. The man with a shriveled hand in Matthew 12:1-14, the crippled woman in Luke 13:10-17, and the man with dropsy in Luke 14:1-6.

45. *A History of the Holy Bible* (Cincinnati: Coleman & Phillips), p. 924. Additional information can be found at https://en.wikipedia.org/wiki/Pool_of_Bethesda (accessed 5/16/2019).

46. Luke 7:11-15.

47. No invitation is included in Luke's report.

48. Matthew 19:16–30.

49. Matthew 12:15 NIV 1984.

50. Some mistakenly suggest that Jesus left because the Pharisees were plotting to kill Him. However, they had already left the scene and were no longer present. Even if they had still been in the vicinity, it would have made little difference as there is no evidence that Jesus ever avoided healing people in order to placate religious leaders.

51. Luke 10:4.

52. Matthew 10:9-10 NKJV.

53. Andrew Arterbury, 'Entertaining Angels: Hospitality in Luke and Acts,' *The Christian Reflection Project* (Waco, TX: Baylor University Press, 2007).

54. Luke 24:17-18.

55. Luke 24:19-24.

56. Luke 24:25-27.

57. Luke 24: 28-29.

58. Luke 24:31-32.

59. Luke 24:33, 35.

60. Comment on Matthew 13:2-3, *New Living Translation Life Application Study Bible* (Wheaton, IL: Tyndale House Publishers, 1996).

61. *Parade Magazine*, February 11, 1962. Also, 'Revelations from the Russian Archives, Anti-Religious Campaigns,' Library of Congress, August 31, 2016 found at https://www.loc.gov/exhibits/archives/anti.html.

62. Luke 10:5-6 NLT.

63. Strong's #2782. *Kerugma* is a noun that derives from the verb *kerusso* and is used to imply the content of what is proclaimed.

SOURCES

64. Acts 16:6-10.

65. Matthew 7:6.

66. Luke 10:10-11.

67. John 3:1-21.

68. Luke 8:1-3.

69. NB: All Pais staff and apprentices are rooted in a local church and become fully functioning members of it.

70. See https://www.bbc.com/news/uk-48054113

71. See Matthew 4:18-22 and Luke 5:1-11.

72. For Biblical references and an in-depth look at the traditional expectations of Jewish hospitality, please see http://jewishencyclopedia.com/articles/7905-hospitality

73. For more of Paul's strategy on reaching the God-fearers, read *In Search of Paul* by John Dominic Crossan and Jonathan L. Reed (San Francisco: HarperOne, 2009).

74. Acts 17:16, 22-23.

75. Acts 17:32 NET.

76. Mark 9:24.

77. Paraphrase of the Arabian Proverb: "Don't pour away your water on the strength of a mirage." Found in book by Martin H. Manser, *The Facts on File Dictionary of Proverbs, 2nd Edition* (New York: Infobase Publishing, 2007), pp. 11.

78. Mark 10:17.

79. Mark 10:21.

80. The Alpha Course is an evangelistic course which introduces the basics of the Christian faith through a series of discussions. You can find out more at https://alpha.org.

81. Referring to the maturing process described by Ephesians 4:13. A full layout of this mainframe is presented in the book, *Talmidim: How to Disciple Anyone in Anything* (Harris House Publishing, 2016), where it explains that the discipleship methods Jesus used pre-existed His incarnation.

82. Dan Kimball, *The Emerging Church* (Grand Rapids, MI: Zondervan, 2003), p. 197.

83. For more on discipling others, see the companion book in this series, *Talmidim: How to Disciple Anyone in Anything* by Paul Clayton Gibbs (Colleyville, TX: Harris House Publishing, 2016).

84. Luke 10:7.

85. John 10:12.

86. Luke 1:10 ISV.

87. Although some translations use the number 72, Messianic scholars believe the correct number is 70. The number 70 is repeated in Scripture (Exodus 24:1; Numbers 11:16; Jeremiah 29:10) and follows a pattern of governance. Note that in 19 BC, the high priest was replaced with the Nasi or 'Prince of the Sanhedrin.' The number 72 is most likely a copyist's error. Also see comment on Luke 10:1 in the *Jewish New Testament Commentary*.

88. The number of members in the Sanhedrin was 70 plus the high priest, making it 71. Jesus, of course, is our High Priest.

89. To discover more of Jesus use of *r'mez*, read the book *Haverim: How to Study Anything with Anyone* (Harris House Publishing, 2013).

90. See https://bible.org/illustration/quote-19

91. In this case, when I say 'Christian,' I mean someone who has accepted Jesus as not just the Messiah but as God, has repented of their sins, and has chosen to make Him Lord of their life.

92. Matthew 16:16.

93. Pastor Derek Smith and his wife Georgina lead King's Church, which has several locations in the North of England. See kingschurchlife.com for more details.

94. 1 Corinthians 2:4.

95. Information on this can be found at https://en.wikipedia.org/wiki/Koha_(custom)

96. Acts 19:13-16.

97. Taken from @Clergycoachingnetwork Facebook post on 28th December 2018.

98. Acts 8:27-31.

99. For a greater understanding of these values read *Post-Modern Pilgrims* (Nashville: B&H Books, 2000) written by Leonard Sweet.

100. Taken from an email I received regarding feedback on my book, *Haverim*.

101. Matthew 7:13-14.

102. For details of these promises, please see the School Charter on the Pais Movement website paismovement.com

103. Ferguson, Alex, *Leading: Learning from Life and My Years at Manchester United* (London: Hodder & Stoughton, 2015), p. 83.

104. Luke 10:1 ISV.

105. Matthew 15:24.

106. 2 Peter 3:9.

107. Luke 10:2.

108. This saying is attributed to the Rev. Robert H. Schuller, who according to *Los Angeles Times*, was most popular for his "pithy and memorable sayings." See https://www.latimes.com/archives/la-xpm-1987-07-18-me-759-story.html accessed 7/11/2019.

SOURCES

109. Acts 4:13.

110. John 9:24-25.

111. John 4:29.

112. This quote is attributed to Joseph Joubert, a French moralist and essayist.

113. Note the shocked reaction of Cleopas as He spoke to Jesus on the road to Emmaus: "Are you the only one visiting Jerusalem who does not know the things that have happened there in these days?" Luke 24:18.

114. Matthew 4:23 NIV 1984.

115. Strong's #1321: pronounced *did-as'-ko*.

116. A popular phrase, this quote, which is often attributed to Francis of Assisi, has no published record before the 1990s.

117. 'Reviving Evangelism' by the Barna Group, a report based on research commissioned by Alpha USA, 2019.

118. Matthew 19:1-2, Mark 10, and Luke 23:5.

119. John 4:40 - also see Luke 17:11-12.

120. Luke 5:6-7.

121. For more details go to www.paismovement.com.

122. All have been created in-house, some in collaboration with my fellow leaders. Mark and Beccy Riley who worked in Northern Ireland for many years and have great experience with prayer for healing on the streets. David Butler is a member of our neighborhood and is the church's Pastoral Director who was already caring for the neighborhood before the church was even planted.

123. Mark 4:8.

124. Acts 16:9-10.

125. Acts 16:13a.

126. Acts 16:13b.

127. Acts 16:14.

128. Acts 16:15.

129. Acts 16:15c.

130. Acts 16:40.

131. Philippians 3:17 NLT.

132. You can find out more at www.becauseyoureloved.com

More about 'Because You're Loved'

My friends Mark and Beccy Riley have served with our organization for over fifteen years. During that time, they led Pais in Northern Ireland and used the Shalom Strategy to create a campaign they called, 'Because You're Loved.'[132] It was successful in getting people to move into intentional acts of kindness that indirectly linked them to the Gospel. Together we re-engineered it for the following two purposes: (1) *To be used everywhere in the world*, and (2) *To be broadened to help people show, share, and bring others to faith.*

The campaign is now used by people all over the world. It is made up of three separate week-long campaigns and teaches people the three parts of mission without the polarizing use of words *or* actions.

'Dared to Love' combines social action with a clear expression of the love of God. Five challenges, or 'dares,' are given to those who participate in the week's mission. Initially, a leader is present to show them how to do it. Each day has a special theme: Day 1 Encouragement; Day 2 Service; Day 3 Compassion; Day 4 Generosity; Day 5 Connection. 'Dared to Love' is used to help people show God's love.

'Who Loves You?' combines a media teaser campaign with an opportunity for people to share their story. Each participant creates a short video in which they tell of God's love using a simple template. They then share this video on their social media for all their friends and family to see. The aim is that they get invited to share more of their story by those who watch it. 'Who Loves You?' is used to help people speak about God's love.

'Bring the Love' combines three special events with a simple tool. An emphasis is placed on not only inviting people somewhere, but actually taking them there. The three events have different themes: Event #1 Social; Event #2 Service; Event #3 Study. 'Bring the Love' is used to help people lead people into God's love.

In many ways the campaign is fairly traditional, but it gets people on the road to sharing their faith. Once they are on the journey, we can begin to train them to do it more like Jesus.

About the Author

Paul Clayton Gibbs is the founder and global director of the Pais Movement. He and his wife Lynn have two sons, Joel and Levi, and have recently become proud grandparents. Originally from Manchester, England, the Gibbs family moved to the USA in 2005 to globally expand Paul's vision of "missionaries making missionaries."

Paul began pioneering openings into Manchester schools as an associate minister in 1987. In September 1992, he founded the Pais Project, initially a one-team gap year project in north Manchester, which has exploded globally, training and placing thousands of missionaries and reaching millions of students throughout Europe, North and South America, Africa, Asia, and Australia. Since then, Paul has pioneered two other branches of Pais: one that equips churches in missional strategies and one that provides businesses with cause marketing strategies. Under Paul's leadership, the Pais Movement continues to grow, launching initiatives and resources to further God's Kingdom.

Paul gained national recognition in the UK for mentoring and training leaders. He has written several books and speaks throughout the world at venues, which include Bible colleges and seminaries, churches, leadership retreats, and youth conferences. His primary topics are pioneering, leadership development, the Kingdom of God, and ancient practices for postmodern times.

Paul enjoys swimming, surfing, skiing, sailing, snowboarding, and is an avid Manchester United fan!

paulgibbs.info
facebook.com/paulcgibbs
twitter.com/paulcgibbs

About the Pais Movement

Our Aim

Pais exists to spark a global movement, where the primary concern of God's people is His Kingdom, and where they are equipped to advance it in their world. We do this through distinctive approaches to mission, discipleship, and study in the areas of youth and schools, churches, and businesses.

Our Passion

Pais is the New Testament Greek word for 'child' or 'child servant to the king.' Our motto is 'missionaries making missionaries.' We are passionate about the people of our world and are desperate to see them in the relationship with God that He intended us to have. We come alongside schools, churches, and businesses in their endeavor to empower people to grow in their understanding and experience of God.

Our Vision

Mission lies at the heart of Pais. We seek to help both the apprentices and those they touch develop missionary hearts, missionary skills, and missionary lives. As each missionary makes a missionary, we see our world change.

paismovement.com
facebook.com/paismovement
twitter.com/paismovement

To learn more about the Pais Movement, watch the documentary.

'THE SPIRIT of a PIONEER'

a film about the four stages of vision

'Inspirational & Informative!'
Based on the book "The Line and the Dot" by Paul Clayton Gibbs

TheSpiritofaPioneerFilm.com
Free to view on

WINDWARD PRODUCTIONS   MAKAKOH IMAGES

FREE MISSION YEAR INCLUDES

200 LECTURE HOURS | **1800** EXPERIENTIAL HOURS
BI-WEEKLY MENTORING | VALUED AT **$10,400**

Choose your course and specialization:

YOUTH
- sports
- music
- performing arts
- personalized

CHURCHES
- church planting
- college ministry
- community outreach

INFRASTRUCTURE
- media
- finance
- training
- communication
- human resources

BUSINESSES
- team coaching
- social responsibility
- company management

apply now!
www.paismovement.com

paismovement | paismovement | paismovement | paismovement

Discover more great resources available through harrishousepublishing.com.

By Karen Sebastian

The Power of Hope for Prodigals
Discover practical steps to establish hope in the midst of dark times. Learn how to see your child through the Father's eyes. Speak words of hope and encouragement. Prepare the way home—it's shorter than you think. Also available in Spanish.

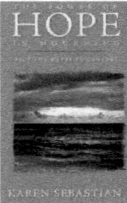

The Power of Hope in Mourning
True grief is often messy, raw, and random, with waves of sadness washing over you. Hope Catalyst Karen Sebastian teaches you to 'ride' the waves, demonstrating how the very pain that threatens to destroy you can push you into the presence of God where hope and healing await.

The Power of Hope for Caregivers
Caring for the needs of a dependent loved one can be overwhelming, but author Karen Sebastian provides hope and perspective to help you serve your loved one well and with no regrets.

By Katie Hopmann

The King's Invitation
Follow the travels of a boy on his journey to see the King. Meeting others along the way, he becomes loaded down with well-meaning gifts and advice. It's a lot to carry! Will he make it to the Royal City?

By Mark Nathan Riley

Because You're Loved
Show the Faith. Share the Faith. Bring the Faith. This simple guide equips groups of believers with the tools to become a catalyst of transformation in their community.

By Paul Clayton Gibbs

The Ancient Trilogy

Haverim
How to help anyone study anything. This unique book takes a 2,000-year-old method of Bible study and gives it a modern twist. Providing step-by-step guidance, Paul Gibbs equips you to launch your own group study using Haverim Devotions.™

Talmidim
How to disciple anyone in anything. Helping us fundamentally rethink our current methods of discipleship, Paul Gibbs gives a fresh understanding of the Great Commission. By researching and applying Jesus's method of discipleship, Gibbs provides a simple template anyone can use.

Shalom
How to reach anyone anywhere. Providing a four-step template used by missionaries around the world, author Paul Gibbs equips you to share your faith with others on both a personal and organizational level.

The Kingdom Trilogy

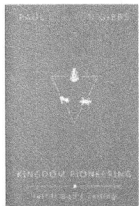

The Kingdom Pioneers
Why do so few of us fulfill our God-given dreams? Do we give up because we think we got it all wrong? In Kingdom Pioneering, author Paul Clayton Gibbs explains how to know if your vision is from God, presents the four stages it will go through, and gives advice to navigate their dangers.

The Kingdom Principles
Debunking the perception that following Christ means following a list of rules, Paul Gibbs unpacks six Kingdom Principles that can transform your relationship with God from a life of rules to one of love.

The Kingdom Patterns
Why does it seem difficult to get a straight answer from God when you are asking for direction? Paul Gibbs presents five diagrams to help you understand where God is leading you and what will happen next. Plus, he offers you a better question to ask.

#shalom

DOWNLOAD THE SHALOM TEMPLATE AT mypais.com

www.ingramcontent.com/pod-product-compliance
Lightning Source LLC
Chambersburg PA
CBHW052058110526
44591CB00013B/2266